THE ROLE OF CENTRAL BANK DIGITAL CURRENCIES IN FINANCIAL INCLUSION

ASIA–PACIFIC FINANCIAL INCLUSION FORUM 2022

ASIAN DEVELOPMENT BANK

ADB

Contents

Tables, Figures, and Case Studies

TABLES

FIGURES

CASE STUDIES

Foreword

Across Asia and the Pacific, technological innovations are enhancing consumer convenience, helping to solve complex problems faster while disrupting traditional business models. In recent years, many economies have invested in new technologies to leverage digital efficiencies—particularly during the COVID-19 pandemic—to foster economic resilience and advance inclusive growth.

Central bank digital currencies (CBDCs) are prominent among these emerging digital solutions. They improve the functioning of the financial sector and, if designed well, expand the range of financial products and services to bring formal financial services to the underbanked and underserved, promoting financial inclusion. CBDCs can lower transaction costs—including for international remittances—build trust in digital services, and provide financial products that better target disadvantaged groups.

As an emerging technology, however, CBDCs carry risks related to cybersecurity, privacy, and financial sector stability, and demand appropriate and effective policy responses to maximize their potential. It is especially important to scrutinize these risks in environments where technical capabilities and infrastructure are less developed.

Asia-Pacific Economic Cooperation (APEC) was founded to promote balanced, inclusive, sustainable, innovative, and secure growth by accelerating regional economic integration and collaboration among its 21 member economies. The Asia–Pacific Financial Inclusion Forum is an APEC initiative that supports this vision. The 2022 forum on "The Role of Central Bank Digital Currencies for Financial Inclusion" helped the region's policy makers to assess the potential benefits of developing CBDCs. It advanced discussion of key policy and regulatory issues, including key design features of CBDCs and suitable legal and regulatory frameworks. It also highlighted critical pre-conditions for success including the inclusion of nonbank service providers and managing risks through effective safeguards. This publication reflects these important discussions.

I am confident that economies interested in developing CBDCs, especially to advance financial inclusion, will value the information and recommendations found in this publication. I hope that knowledge products such as this one created as part of the Asia–Pacific Financial Inclusion Forum initiative will inspire regional policy makers and advance regional cooperation to support APEC's vision of a prosperous and equitable future for all.

Albert Park
Chief Economist and Director General
Economic Research and Regional Cooperation Department
Asian Development Bank

Acknowledgments

This publication was prepared by the Asian Development Bank (ADB), Regional Cooperation and Integration Division (ERCI) of the Economic Research and Regional Cooperation Department (ERCD) under the overall guidance and supervision of Cyn-Young Park, director, ERCI. The ADB Technical Assistance 9922: Strengthening Regional Cooperation and Knowledge Sharing on the Application of Technology in Financial Services supported this project.

Shawn Hunter (industry fellow and director, inclusive growth programs, Griffith Asia Institute); Robert Bianchi (professor of finance and director of the Griffith Centre for Personal Finance and Superannuation, Griffith University); Akihiro Omura (lecturer of finance, Department of Accounting, Finance and Economics, Griffith University); Victor Wong (senior lecturer of finance, Department of Accounting, Finance and Economics, Griffith University); and Rolando Avendano (economist, ERCI, ADB) are the main authors of this publication.

The publication greatly benefited from the discussions at the 12th annual Asia–Pacific Financial Inclusion Forum policy dialogue, which was held virtually on 17 June 2022, in collaboration with APEC Business Advisory Council and the Asian Development Bank Institute (ADBI), with implementation support from the Griffith Asia Institute. The following forum speakers are acknowledged for their support for this publication: Richard Robinson (chief strategist, open data and standards, Bloomberg); Ross Buckley (KPMG Law – King & Wood Mallesons professor of disruptive innovation, and a Scientia Professor, UNSW Sydney); Bernard Yeung (Stephen Riady Distinguished Professor in finance and strategic management, National University of Singapore Business School, and president, Asian Bureau of Finance and Economics Research); Satoru Yamadera (advisor, ERCD, ADB); Jermy Prenio (principal advisor, Financial Stability Institute, Bank for International Settlements); Xiongwu Luo (deputy manager, Digital Currency and Anti-counterfeiting Management Division, Currency, Gold and Silver Bureau, People's Bank of China); Edna Villa (assistant governor, Currency Development Sub-Sector, Bangko Sentral ng Pilipinas); Kasidit Tansanguan (director, Corporate Strategy Department and head, Digital Currency Team, Bank of Thailand); and Suvendu Pati (chief general manager, Reserve Bank of India).

Helpful comments received from Julius Caesar Parreñas (senior advisor, Daiwa Institute of Research Ltd at Daiwa Securities Group) and Peter Morgan (senior consulting economist, vice chair of Research, ADBI) are gratefully acknowledged.

ADBI staff who supported the organization and conduct of the forum include Pitchaya Sirivunnabood (deputy head of capacity building and training and senior capacity building and training economist), Midori Sato (administrative assistant), and Preechaya Kittipaisalsilpa (capacity building and training associate).

An earlier version of the publication was submitted to APEC Finance Ministers in October 2022. Rolando Avendano and Paulo Rodelio Halili (senior economics officer, ERCI, ADB) coordinated the production of this publication, with support from Marilyn Parra (senior operations assistant, ERCI, ADB).

Eric Van Zant edited the manuscript, Francis Manio created the cover design, and Alvin Tubio implemented the typesetting and layout. Maria Guia de Guzman proofread the publication, while Levi Lusterio handled the page proof checking, with assistance from Carol Ongchangco and Paulo Rodelio Halili. The Printing Services Unit of ADB's Corporate Services Department and the Publishing Team of the Department of Communications supported printing and publishing.

Abbreviations

ADB	Asian Development Bank
ADBI	Asian Development Bank Institute
APEC	Asia–Pacific Economic Cooperation
APFIF	Asia–Pacific Financial Inclusion Forum
BIS	Bank for International Settlements
CBDC	central bank digital currency
COVID-19	coronavirus disease
DLT	distributed ledger technology
fintech	financial technology
G20	Group of 20
KYC	know-your-customer
MSMEs	micro, small, and medium-sized enterprises

Executive Summary

As digital transformation accelerates globally, new innovative technology solutions to enhance financial inclusion are being developed more rapidly than ever. The development of cryptocurrency markets, and their growing popularity among consumers, has generated significant interest among governments globally in exploring the prospect of central bank-issued digital currencies—as a mechanism that could leverage digital finance technologies and as infrastructure to enhance the reach and value of formal financial products and services among the unbanked or underserved. However, as an emerging technology, considerable uncertainty remains about what is "best practice" in the development and implementation of a central bank digital currency (CBDC). This includes the specific design features that will enhance a CBDC's impact on financial inclusion.

In response, the Asian Development Bank and its partners in the Asia–Pacific Financial Inclusion Forum have examined the potential role of CBDCs as a driver of financial inclusion and identified several key priorities and recommendations for governments pursuing or interested in this technology to help ensure it achieves the desired impact.

The Asia–Pacific Financial Inclusion Forum is a policy initiative of the Asia–Pacific Economic Cooperation Finance Ministers' Process. It was proposed by the APEC Business Advisory Council to identify actions that policy makers and regulators can take to put financial services within the reach of the underserved.

Central Bank Digital Currency and Its Applications

In basic terms, a CBDC can be defined as a digital currency which is the liability of a central bank. However, because it can be designed to deliver multiple functions and purposes, a standard definition of a CBDC is not straightforward, since the term can be used to describe a wide variety of potential digital currencies. Notwithstanding this degree of variability, some basic elements might be considered consistent or common components of a CBDC. These include that a CBDC is a form of central bank money that is a store of value and employed as a medium of exchange, and for a retail CBDC, creates the potential for a direct relationship between the central bank and the general public.

When designing a CBDC, governments need to consider several potential features and functions. Some key examples include issuing a CBDC with custodial or noncustodial settings, whether ownership of the currency is verified through an account or token-based system, or determining what parties can access it as a wholesale or retail currency. These different design features and functions of a CBDC can significantly impact its potential to address market needs, including financial inclusion, and represent some of the critical issues governments will face to ensure their design fits local needs and priorities.

Key infrastructure requirements also greatly impact design and effective implementation of a CBDC. This includes basic infrastructure such as stable electricity, access to smart phones, internet coverage, and a functional digital identity system. Determining what infrastructure and technology are most important for a CBDC that can drive financial inclusion first requires understanding consumer needs, which will differ between economies.

Potential Role of Central Bank Digital Currencies: Opportunities and Challenges of Central Bank Digital Currency for Financial Inclusion

The COVID-19 pandemic has brought greater attention to the role of digital financial products and services in serving the needs of vulnerable populations, particularly as a mechanism for building greater resilience to economic shocks. As such, interest has grown in the viability of CBDCs as a successful driver of financial inclusion; indeed, it has become a primary reason for exploring or piloting a CBDC among many governments.

Specific benefits to financial inclusion through a CBDC have been identified, even if it may be too early to determine how well a CBDC will address the constraints limiting the reach and use of formal financial products and services among the unserved or underserved. These benefits include:

- enhancing access to finance for micro, small, and medium-sized enterprises;
- enabling greater consumer confidence or trust in digital financial services;
- streamlining the small-value digital transaction system;
- reducing the cost of financial transactions;
- enhancing the value of financial services through superior data collection and application of tailored services; and
- enhancing efficiency in financial transactions.

On the other hand, implementing a CBDC is not simple. It brings new risks and unique challenges that governments will need to manage to ensure it achieves financial inclusion, especially in developing or emerging markets where technical capability or infrastructure may fall short. A CBDC will likely experience many of the same challenges that traditional digital financial services have faced in expanding reach and usage among the disadvantaged. Such groups face common constraints including inadequate or unreliable infrastructure, lack of access to required hardware, limited digital literacy or capabilities, lack of awareness, or continued reliance on the traditional cash economy.

Governments also face potential negative impacts on the broader financial system in implementing CBDCs for financial inclusion. One such concern is whether a CBDC might undermine the stability of the financial system if consumer demand for the CBDC outpaces demand for traditional currencies, potentially resulting in unintended consequences, such as bank solvency and liquidity problems.

Potential competition between a CBDC and traditional financial products and services offered by conventional banks is another concern. Clearly, impacts that threaten the stability of the financial system can constrain the effectiveness of financial inclusion measures.

Connecting Central Bank Digital Currencies with the Existing Financial System to Improve Financial Inclusion

There is no single pathway by which a CBDC can connect to the local economy or the global financial system. As a digital alternative to cash, a CBDC can be integrated with the existing financial system as a widely accepted medium of exchange and store of value. If a CBDC is to have a meaningful impact on financial inclusion, there are a number of important considerations in how it is integrated into the existing financial system.

In all of this, several critical components are required as part of the CBDC design. These include ensuring a secure and reliable system is in place for determining the digital identity of the person transacting. This feature would allow central banks to manage know-your-customer (KYC) processes. Payment systems are another important consideration. The ability to connect the CBDC into an existing and robust digital payments system will significantly enhance the functionality of the currency. Finally, interoperability is a crucial feature with potentially significant impact on support for financial inclusion, particularly as higher interoperability could lead to greater adoption and usage of the CBDC.

Recommendations for Policy Makers and Regulators

(i) **Consider which CBDC design features will be most effective for financial inclusion by:**

- determining if desired CBDC design features would be recognized and impacted by current policies and regulations and any potential unforeseen policy or regulatory challenges which could impact financial inclusion issues;

- weighing the costs and benefits of a CBDC against other solutions for addressing financial inclusion, including alternative innovative technologies that may be less resource intensive; and

- pursuing collaborations with other governments in the region, including joint assessments, to understand and address cross-border implications of a CBDC, including how the currency could be recognized in different jurisdictions in the case of international remittances.

(ii) **Prioritize addressing the required preconditions for a successful digital financial inclusion by:**

- leveraging the existing system of regulated financial intermediaries to distribute a CBDC and provide access channels;

- addressing onerous identification and KYC requirements, especially for small transactions, by integrating a CBDC with a domestic digital identification system, simplifying due diligence requirements through reforms, and promoting remote onboarding or e-KYC methods;

- addressing financial and digital literacy and consumer protection needs by taking an active role in building awareness, level of skills, and trust in digital financial services through campaigns and public–private partnerships targeting disadvantaged segments of the population; and

- fostering interoperability among multiple dimensions, including digital payment and settlement systems, to enhance the viability of a CBDC to be a suitable currency option for all members of society and drive the adoption of a digital payment and settlement systems.

(iii) **Recognize and manage the risks associated with the introduction of a CBDC by:**

- establishing safeguards to mitigate potentially negative CBDC impacts on finance sector stability by crowding out or directly competing with the commercial banking sector and financial services industry; and

- investing in cybersecurity technology and capabilities, including consumer protection policies and education programs, to enable adequate protection for CBDC users against potential risks including fraud, privacy breaches, human error, and others.

Introduction

The Asia–Pacific Financial Inclusion Forum (APFIF) is an Asia–Pacific Economic Cooperation (APEC) initiative established in 2010 to support the extension of formal financial products and services to the unbanked and underserved. The initiative provides a platform for policy makers, regulators, development experts, and industry leaders to take an active role in identifying, developing, and validating concrete policy recommendations and promoting them through official APEC channels. Following more than a decade of implementation, APFIF has established itself as a preeminent program that has successfully supported policy reform and built the capacity of governments to meet the challenges associated with financial inclusion.

Digital transformation is increasingly important in achieving financial inclusion goals. The World Bank's latest Global Findex Report data indicate that account ownership worldwide has increased by 50% over the past 10 years. Much of this success is being attributed to the rise of financial technology (fintech) and digital financial services, which have the potential to overcome many traditional access barriers through lower costs, greater convenience, and tailored products and services that better meet consumer needs. The Findex data points out the importance of digital payments and mobile money as a catalyst for use of other digitally enabled financial services and bridging gender gaps. It has also highlighted the impact of the coronavirus disease (COVID-19) pandemic in boosting adoption of digital financial products and services, with over 40% of adults in developing countries[1] making a digital merchant payment for the first time at the start of the pandemic. However, despite this success, nearly 30% of adults in developing economies remain financially excluded (Demirgüç-Kunt et al. 2022).

As digital transformation accelerates, governments and industry pursue innovation to continue the expansion of formal account ownership and usage and to deepen the use of broader financial products and services that can provide valuable benefits to those at the base of the economy.[2] Central bank digital currencies (CBDCs) are one of the innovations gaining significant interest in recent years, especially for financial inclusion.

---

[1] Excluding the People's Republic of China.

[2] "Base of the economy" refers to the poorest socioeconomic segment, including individuals, households, and the microenterprises they operate.

In 2022, the APFIF initiative, under the APEC Finance Minsters' Process, has focused on this emerging technology to provide greater clarity and guidance on the opportunities and risks of CBDCs, specifically their potential impact on financial inclusion. Issues explored through the APFIF initiative include:

- understanding CBDCs and their applications,

- opportunities and challenges associated with CBDCs as a driver for financial inclusion, and

- connecting CBDCs to the existing financial system to enable financial inclusion.

These efforts align with several key priorities of APEC, including the Putrajaya Vision 2040, which promotes action toward greater prosperity through inclusive growth and development. It also includes the priorities of APEC's Host Economy for 2022, Thailand, and its theme for the year *"Open. Connect. Balance"* which calls for resilient, inclusive, balanced, and sustainable growth for the region.

This publication reviews these topics and recommends actions for policy makers and regulators identified through a policy dialogue convened through the APFIF initiative on 17 June 2022 under the theme *"The Role of Central Bank Digital Currencies in Financial Inclusion."*

The Asian Development Bank leads the APFIF in cooperation with the Asian Development Bank Institute, with implementation support from the Griffith Asia Institute. It is one of three platforms for collaboration among the public and private sectors and multilateral institutions whose general oversight is entrusted to APEC Business Advisory Council.[3]

---

[3]   The other two are the Asia–Pacific Financial Forum, established in 2013, and the Asia-Pacific Infrastructure Partnership, established in 2011.

1 Central Bank Digital Currency and its Applications

The term central bank digital currency (CBDC) has emerged as an overarching phrase to describe a wide variety of potential digital currencies. A unifying definition of a CBDC is not straightforward, because it can be designed to deliver multiple functions and purposes. However, in basic terms it can be defined as a digital currency which is the liability of a central bank. For example, a CBDC can be developed for interbank payment functions only, with no interaction with the general public, i.e., "wholesale." On the other hand, a CBDC may be designed to be used by the retail public to enhance overall well-being and to connect disadvantaged individuals into the electronic banking and payments system. Importantly, a CBDC has the potential to bring more people into the formal financial system and thus play a role in enhancing financial inclusion across the broader population.

To understand CBDCs, it is important to first examine the various descriptions that have been used to illustrate the various features and functions of this innovative financial concept. Table 1 provides examples of these descriptions from different institutions.

Table 1: Central Bank Digital Currency Descriptions

Bank for International Settlements (BIS): *"CBDC is not a well-defined term. It is used to refer to a number of concepts. However, it is envisioned by most to be a new form of central bank money. That is, a central bank liability, denominated in an existing unit of account, which serves both as a medium of exchange and a store of value. This would be an innovation for general purpose users but not for wholesale entities. Central banks already provide digital money in the form of reserves or settlement account balances held by commercial banks and certain other financial institutions at the central bank. This mix of new and already existing forms of central bank money makes it challenging to precisely define what a CBDC is. In fact, for purposes of analyzing what may change, it is easier to define a CBDC by highlighting what it is not: a CBDC is a digital form of central bank money that is different from balances in traditional reserve or settlement accounts."* [a]

US Federal Reserve: *"A CBDC is a digital form of central bank money that is widely available to the general public. 'Central bank money' refers to money that is a liability of the central bank. In the United States, there are currently two types of central bank money: physical currency issued by the Federal Reserve and digital balances held by commercial banks at the Federal Reserve. While Americans have long held money predominantly in digital form—for example in bank accounts, payment apps or through online transactions—a CBDC would differ from existing digital money available to the general public because a CBDC would be a liability of the Federal Reserve, not of a commercial bank."* [b]

Bank of England: *"A Central Bank Digital Currency (CBDC) would be an electronic form of central bank money that could be more widely used by households and businesses to make payments and store value. CBDC is sometimes thought of as equivalent to a digital banknote, although in practice it may have other features that will depend on its final design."* [c]

CBDC = central bank digital currency, US = United States.

[a] Bank for International Settlements (BIS). 2018. *Central Bank Digital Currencies*. Committee on Payments and Market Infrastructures – Markets Committee. March. pp. 3–4.

[b] Board of Governors of the Federal Reserve System. 2022. *What is a Central Bank Digital Currency?*

[c] Bank of England. 2020. Central Bank Digital Currency Opportunities, Challenges and Design. *Discussion Paper.* London. March. p. 7.

Table 1 descriptions suggest no formal or universally accepted definition of a CBDC. Yet, some basic elements might be considered consistent or common components of a CBDC:

- CBDC is regarded as a complementary and/or supplementary form of physical currency that represents a store of physical currency in a digital format. This idea is similar to the use of cryptocurrencies; however, it entails less fluctuation as it is held and traded by known owners.

- Nearly every description of CBDCs suggests this new central bank money will be employed as a *medium of exchange*. This commonality suggests that CBDCs can be employed to facilitate the transactions of goods and services between counterparties.

- CBDC would enable automation of clearing house and decentralized netting payment settlement between banks (in a wholesale CBDC structure), reducing risk of collateralization and cost efficiencies. This would reduce costs to the general public (in a retail CBDC setting).

The following sections summarize key CBDC features and functions, with emphasis on elements which could enhance financial inclusion.

Central Bank Digital Currency versus Cryptocurrency

From the outset, it may appear that a CBDC and cryptocurrency are quite similar as it is sometimes difficult to differentiate between the two. The obvious advantage of a CBDC over cryptocurrency is that it is issued by a known authority (central bank) and therefore, it is regulated and can assist with decisions such as monetary policy. Furthermore, the value of a CBDC is expected to be linked to the respective economy's currency, and thus, complements the current menu of currency instruments available (e.g., cash and savings in bank accounts at commercial banks). As a result, it is expected the price volatility and fluctuations in CBDCs will be lower and more stable than what is experienced in cryptocurrency markets.

Features and Functions of a Central Bank Digital Currency

Custodial versus Noncustodial

A CBDC may be issued with either custodial or noncustodial features. A CBDC with custodial settings means that the central bank (or its agents such as commercial banks) hold responsibility for the security aspects of the holders of CBDCs (i.e., identification, security, private keys, passwords, etc.). A CBDC with noncustodial settings means that the individual user carries full responsibility for the ownership, private keys, and passwords for the CBDC they own. This means users with noncustodial settings are at higher risk as the wealth stored in a CBDC may be permanently lost (due to forgotten passwords or private keys) with no recourse to a third party. In the interests of financial inclusion, there may be a stronger interest by central banks to provide CBDCs with custodial settings to the most financial vulnerable to ensure their savings in a CBDC wallet are not lost or stolen as they may lack financial or digital literacy.

Account-based versus Token-based

In broad terms, CBDCs are often categorized as either account-based or token-based. One of the main differences between the two is how the ownership of CBDCs is verified.

In an account-based system, ownership of the CBDC is recorded in a database and verified through an identification process of the claimed owner (Auer and Böhme 2020a). By contrast, transactions of token-based CBDCs are verified by matching public and private key cryptography like conventional cryptocurrencies. Under this model, a user's identity is not required in verification. A public key (or a shorter/hushed version of it) is akin to someone's street address provided to the public which is created from a private key. A CBDC owned by someone is related to this person's public key but the ownership can be verified only by this person's private key used in creating the public key. This pairing process ensures high levels of privacy but also creates greater difficulties for tracing money laundering and fraudulent transactions (Deloitte 2020).

Transactions of token-based CBDCs can be verified through several different approaches. One is a process called "proof of work"—which is a decentralized mechanism where a transaction is verified by participating members of a network. Alternatively, a "proof of stake" mechanism is where a transaction is validated by parties called validators. Transactions can also be consummated through a centrally distributed model where transactions are verified by a single entity (Sridhar and Horan 2021). Figure 1 explains how accounts are verified in token and account-based CBDCs.

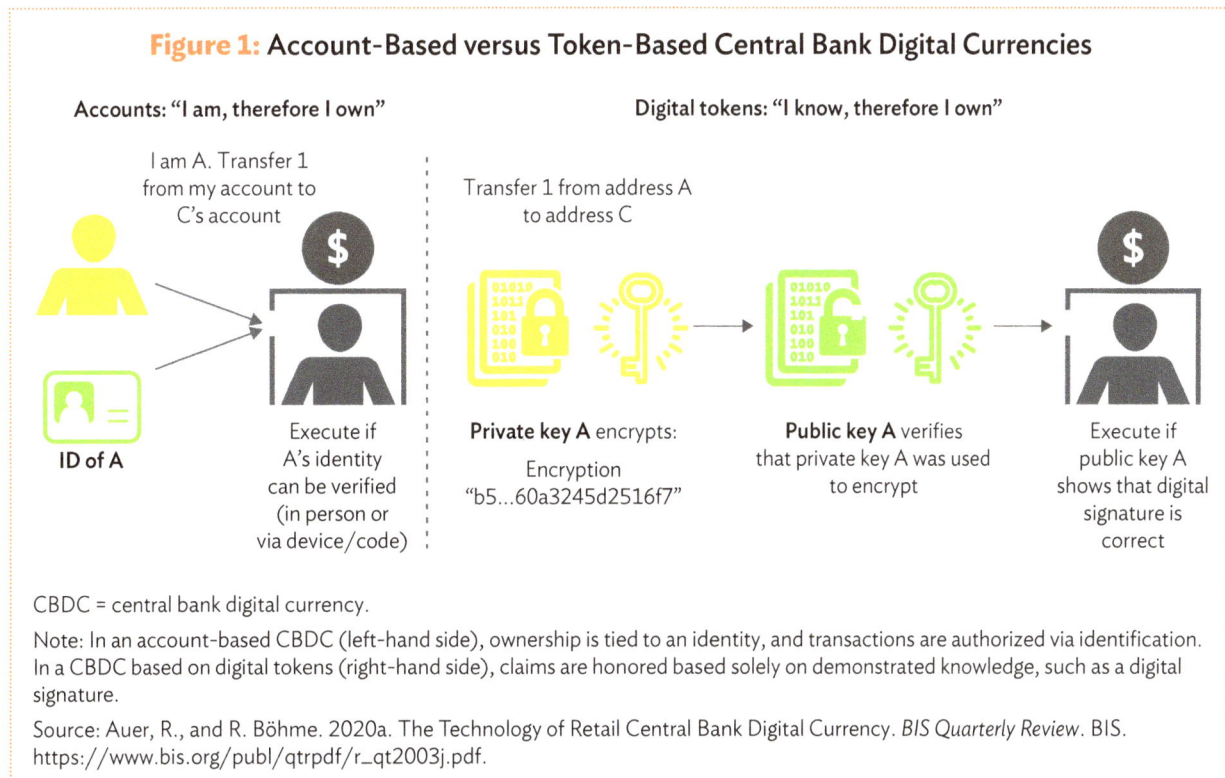

Figure 1: Account-Based versus Token-Based Central Bank Digital Currencies

Accounts: "I am, therefore I own"

Digital tokens: "I know, therefore I own"

I am A. Transfer 1 from my account to C's account

Transfer 1 from address A to address C

ID of A

Execute if A's identity can be verified (in person or via device/code)

Private key A encrypts:
Encryption "b5...60a3245d2516f7"

Public key A verifies that private key A was used to encrypt

Execute if public key A shows that digital signature is correct

CBDC = central bank digital currency.

Note: In an account-based CBDC (left-hand side), ownership is tied to an identity, and transactions are authorized via identification. In a CBDC based on digital tokens (right-hand side), claims are honored based solely on demonstrated knowledge, such as a digital signature.

Source: Auer, R., and R. Böhme. 2020a. The Technology of Retail Central Bank Digital Currency. *BIS Quarterly Review*. BIS. https://www.bis.org/publ/qtrpdf/r_qt2003j.pdf.

Token-based CBDCs offer several advantages over account-based. For example, token-based CBDCs enable easier cross-border transactions, and anonymity can be higher than that of account-based CBDCs. At the same time, these features can lead to money laundering and financial terrorism activities, as pointed out by international organizations in recent policy discussions on general cryptoassets (OECD 2020).

Token-based CBDCs also ensure universal access as anybody can obtain a digital signature (Auer and Böhme 2020a). Transactions can also be executed offline, although periodic access to a network is still required. One example is transferring the CBDC stored on a mobile device to another device using wireless technologies (Richards, Thompson, and Dark 2020). Nevertheless, token-based CBDC transactions tend to be slower than account-based CBDCs. Token-based CBDCs may also be more susceptible to hacking, especially if the central bank employs a decentralized network model (Sridhar and Horan 2021). Table 2 compares the key features of account-based and token-based CBDCs.

Table 2: Comparison of Account-Based and Token-Based Central Bank Digital Currency Systems

Points of Comparison	Account-Based	Token-Based
Cross-system portability and synchronization	Difficult	Easy
Transaction traceability	Difficult	No
Complexity to implement transaction anonymity	High	Low
Cross-border payments	Difficult	Easy
Enable universal access	No	Yes
Offline transactions	No	Yes
Custodial versus noncustodial	Custodial	Usually noncustodial

Source: Adapted from Chan, Aldar C-F. 2021. *UTXO in Digital Currencies: Account-Based or Token-Based? Or Both?* University of Hong Kong. https://arxiv.org/pdf/2109.09294.pdf.

Although the literature tends to categorize CBDCs as either account or token-based, Garratt et al. (2020) argue that some CBDCs may actually be classified as both account-based and token-based. Using Bitcoin as an example, they argue that requiring a private key in a transaction is analogous to proving the identity of the party and thereby satisfies the definition of an account-based cryptocurrency. They also argue that verifying the validity of the amount of Bitcoin possessed by tracing the history of the Bitcoin being transacted satisfies the definition of token-based cryptocurrency. This ambiguity highlights the difficulties associated with designing a CBDC and the need for governments to allow for adequate flexibility rather than attempting to rely on what might be considered a firm definition.

One consideration in the design of a CBDC is the resources required to maintain and monitor the account-based or token-based architecture. Recent studies by Cambridge (2022) suggest the electricity usage required to maintain various private-sector based digital tokens (e.g., Bitcoin) may not be consistent with efficient energy use. Two dimensions of energy cost can be considered: first, that it shifts the energy cost onto the CBDC and thus increases the implied cost of using a CBDC if it uses a decentralized ledger system.

Second, from a financial inclusion perspective, an issue is whether the most financially vulnerable can employ CBDCs if the implied energy cost is passed to them in some form (i.e., in overall pricing, transaction costs, or other form of additional expenditure). A new CBDC must consider these design features to enable and enhance the currency's potential to successfully drive financial inclusion.

Wholesale versus Retail

CBDCs can also be categorized by characteristics of the parties who can access them. In particular, a CBDC that is circulated only by banks and other market participants is considered a wholesale CBDC, while a CBDC that individuals can access is considered a retail CBDC.

Wholesale CBDCs will be used for the settlement of transactions in wholesale markets such as purchases of financial assets or conducting interbank transfers (Bank of International Settlements [BIS] 2021b; Richards, Thompson, and Dark 2020). In this way, wholesale CBDCs will likely play a similar role as reserves held at central banks. However, unlike reserves, some additional functions can be added to wholesale CBDCs. For example, CBDC transactions can be automated by imposing a function that executes transactions if predefined conditions are met (BIS 2021b). Another advantage of wholesale CBDCs would be the cost and the speed of executing cross-border payments (BIS Innovation Hub 2022).

Several central bank groups have explored a wholesale system that facilitates cross-border transactions. This includes a study conducted by the BIS Innovation Hub Singapore Centre, Reserve Bank of Australia, Bank Negara Malaysia, the Monetary Authority of Singapore, and the South African Reserve Bank, which is exploring a common platform for multiple CBDCs (BIS Innovation Hub 2022). Through this study, participating central banks issue their own CBDCs denominated in their own domestic currency with participating commercial banks carrying the CBDCs directly. Figure 2 illustrates the transactions of these CBDCs that are facilitated within a common settlement platform. The platform allows participating parties to access foreign currencies without possessing accounts in the correspondent banks. While the study has identified various benefits, the group has also identified critical challenges. These include allowing foreign banks which do not operate in a host economy to provide financial services there, jurisdictional boundaries that arise from different payments regulations, and allowing foreign central banks to take part in governing domestic payments systems.

With retail CBDCs, many transactions would occur between individuals and businesses. For this reason, transactions tend to be low in value but large in volume (Deloitte 2020). Retail CBDCs therefore can be treated like a digital version of cash that is essentially universally accessible. Figure 3 visualizes the owner's claims on cash, retail CBDCs, and bank deposits. Cash and retail CBDCs have direct claims on the central bank, while claims on bank deposits go through commercial banks. As banks lend out a considerable percentage of funds that customers deposit, there is a risk of the customers' claims not being fully honored (Auer and Böhme 2020b). This implies that if people use CBDCs as a means of storing their value, the balance sheet of central banks may increase substantially while the crowding out of commercial banks' deposits may occur if CBDCs are introduced (Fernandez-Villaverde et al. 2021).

Figure 2: The Multiple Central Bank Digital Currency Platform

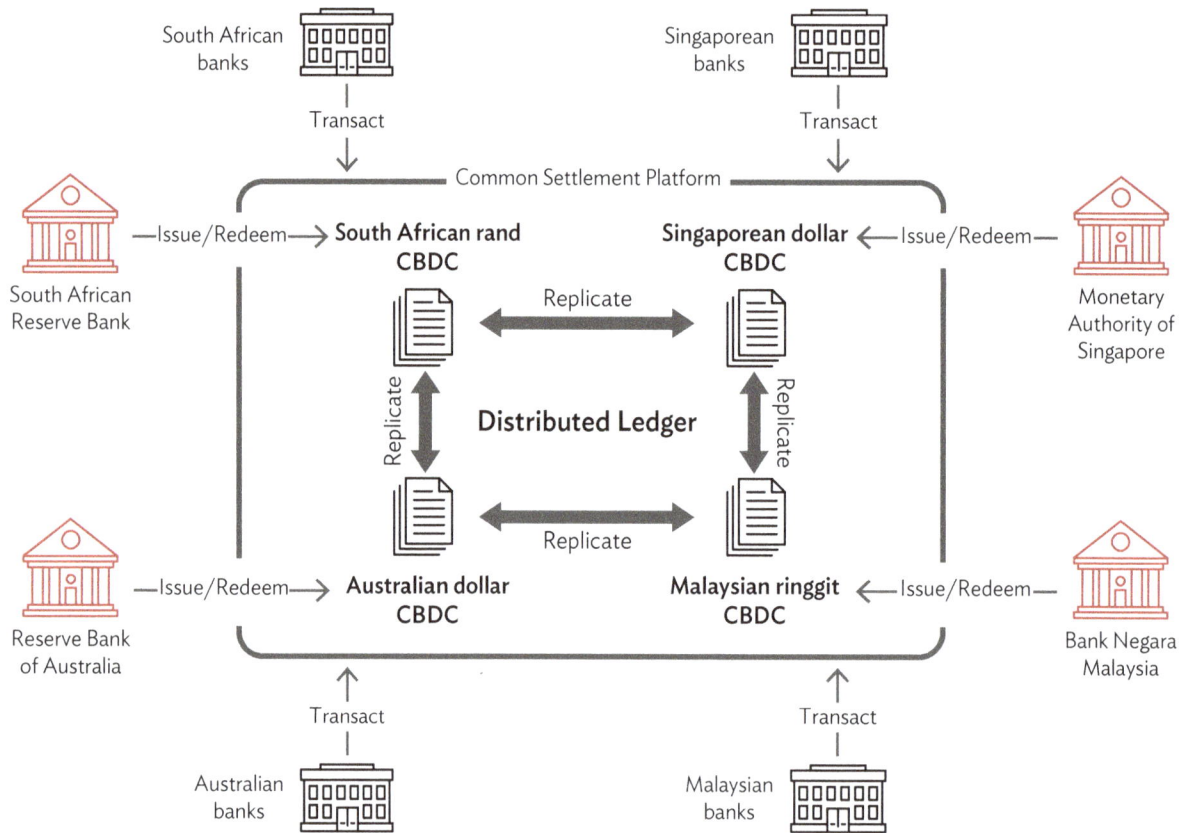

CBDC = central bank digital currency.
Source: BIS Innovation Hub. 2022. *International Settlements Using Multi-CBDCs.* https://www.bis.org/publ/othp47.pdf.

Figure 3: Cash, Electronic Payment Instruments, and Retail Central Bank Digital Currency

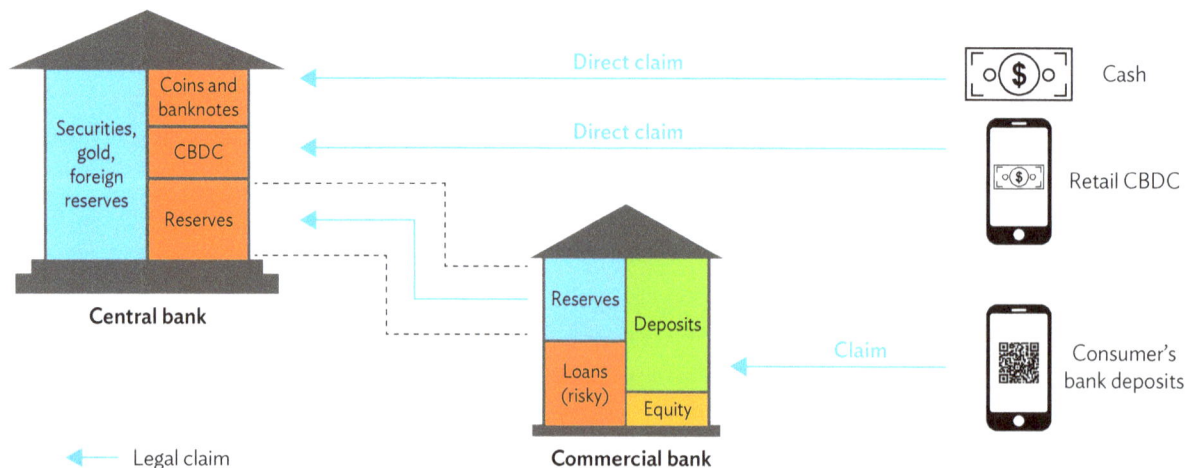

CBDC = central bank digital currency.
Source: Auer, R., and R. Böhme. 2020b. Central Bank Digital Currency: The Quest for Minimally Invasive Technology. *BIS Working Papers.* No. 948. Basel: BIS. https://www.bis.org/publ/work948.pdf.

Case Study 1: Wholesale Central Bank Digital Currency Pilot Program in the Philippines

One of the major objectives of the Bangko Sentral ng Pilipinas (BSP) in contributing to the development of a more sustainable economy is to transform the Philippine financial system to a more technologically advanced and more inclusive system. Internally, the central bank of the Philippines undertakes capacity building activities to ensure the institution is abreast of fast-evolving technologies that drive the emergence of alternative payment instruments such as central bank digital currencies (CBDCs).

In 2020, the BSP conducted a comprehensive exploratory study to determine and evaluate the issues that surround CBDC issuance based on literature and learnings of other central banks. The prospective implications for the pillars of central banking in the Philippines, legal aspects, as well as the potential of CBDCs in furthering financial inclusion were documented in a study entitled *Central Bank Digital Currency for the BSP: Fundamentals and Strategies.*[a] Among other major findings, the study notes that the issuance of a Philippine retail CBDC (rCBDC) cannot be accommodated under existing Philippine legal and regulatory frameworks.

In 2021, the BSP further studied the value-added benefits of issuing a Philippine CBDC by comparing the functional features of the economy's retail and large-value payment systems with the use of CBDCs. It concluded that:

(i)   There is minimal value-added benefit for the use of rCBDC in the Philippines in the short term given the progress of widespread implementation of retail payment digitalization and financial inclusion reforms; and

(ii) There may be value in a wholesale CBDC (wCBDC) in addressing the "pain points" in the domestic payment system of: (a) frictions on cross-border foreign currency transfers, (b) settlement risk exposure arising from the use of commercial bank money in the local equities market, and (c) challenge of operating an intraday liquidity facility that is yet to be automated end-to-end. Enhancing cross-border payments efficiency and safety is a top agenda, with the Philippines being a top recipient of global remittances. Meanwhile, reducing the settlement time for stock market transactions can enhance financial market depth, liquidity, and price discovery, thereby encouraging more individuals and institutional investors to participate in the domestic capital markets.

In 2022, the BSP plans to conduct a pilot wCBDC under the initiative dubbed as the Project CBDCPh to have hands-on knowledge on the functionality, architectural, technological, operational, and organizational requirements of a CBDC. The pilot shall experiment on how a wCBDC may allow 24/7 settlement of large-value transactions (i.e., during off-business hours), which in the Philippines, include the clearing settlement of retail payments. The learnings from this pilot shall serve as critical inputs in the crafting of the medium to long-term road map of the BSP in pursuing further CBDC projects aimed to enhance the domestic payment system.

[a] Bangko Sentral ng Pilipinas. 2021. *Central Bank Digital Currency for the BSP: Fundamentals and Strategies.* https://www.bsp.gov.ph/Media_And_Research/Publications/CBDC_for_the_BSP_Book.pdf.
Source: Authors.

The Value of Central Bank Digital Currencies Against Fiat Currency

The value of CBDCs can be determined in either nominal or real terms. If a central bank wishes to stabilize its CBDC's nominal value (e.g., 1 CBDC = $1), Bordo and Levin (2017) argue that the total value of such currency will remain quite stable when nominal interest rates are positive as individuals and businesses are less inclined to possess the CBDC more than necessary.

However, when the nominal interest rate is negative, individuals and businesses would be more inclined to possess CBDCs and convert their funds into the CBDC, which would pay zero interest. This weakens the effect of monetary policy (Bordo and Levin 2017), and thereby, the CBDC may be no better than conventional cash in stimulating demand.

However, if the central bank decides to implement the official interest rate mechanism via the CBDC, monetary policy can be transmitted through society more directly and effectively (Ward and Rochemont 2019). The price of CBDCs (like treasury bills) would be influenced by monetary policy if the central bank pays interest (Sridhar and Horan 2021), thereby improving the effectiveness of monetary policy, while this introduces competition between CBDCs and conventional bank deposits. This is especially the case when the nominal interest rate is positive. By contrast, a negative interest rate triggered by an adverse economic shock would incentivize individuals and businesses to convert CBDC into cash (an asset that pays zero interest). This makes monetary policies less effective. To overcome this challenge, Bordo and Levin (2017) recommend imposing fees on exchanging cash for a CBDC (and vice versa).

The value of CBDCs could also be altered based on the changes in the general price level (e.g., peg with the consumer price index), while maintaining a constant nominal value is adopted by the majority of the central banks. In this case, the central bank can simply reflect the fluctuation of the price level (both up and down), or the value can be altered asymmetrically depending on the direction of the price level change. For example, similar to the United States Treasury Inflation-Protected Securities, the nominal value of CBDCs can be increased when the consumer price index is higher than a predetermined target, while no adjustment is made when the price level drops (Bordo and Levin 2017).

Key Infrastructure Requirements

Essential critical infrastructure is needed for a CBDC to be a viable currency in the market. To decide what infrastructure/technology are required, the needs of consumers must first be understood. From there, the necessary technology components can be designed to fulfill the purpose of CBDC to enhance financial inclusion.

To assist, a revised version of the Auer and Böhme (2020a) CBDC pyramid has been adapted, to outline the various design choices in developing a CBDC (Figure 4). To successfully rollout a CBDC, the economy should have adequate basic infrastructure in place, such as stable electricity, access to smart phones, good internet coverage, and a functional digital identity system (the **Basic infrastructure** box in Figure 4). Next, the design of CBDC should consider whether there are linkages between a wholesale CBDC and a retail CBDC (Interlinkages box) as discussed in the earlier section of the report. Subsequently, the consideration of whether a CBDC should be account-based or token-based (Access box).

Figure 4: Central Bank Digital Currency Pyramid for Design Choices to Meet Consumer Needs

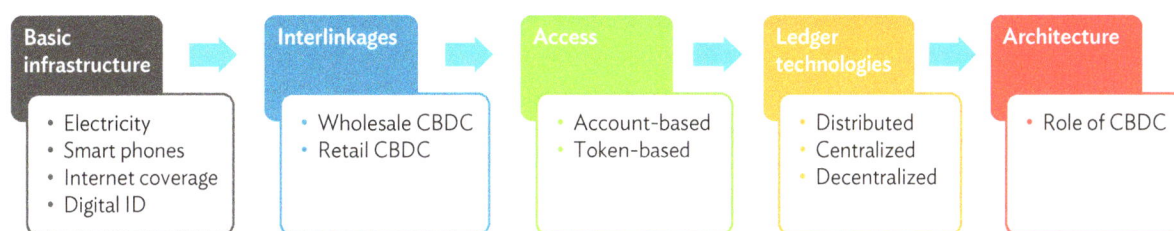

Basic infrastructure	Interlinkages	Access	Ledger technologies	Architecture
• Electricity • Smart phones • Internet coverage • Digital ID	• Wholesale CBDC • Retail CBDC	• Account-based • Token-based	• Distributed • Centralized • Decentralized	• Role of CBDC

CBDC = central bank digital currency.

Source: Adapted from Auer and Böhme (2020a).

The deployment of ledger technology infrastructures (Ledger technologies box) includes considerations such as servers, network access, and whether the CBDC will employ a distributed ledger technology (DLT) platform or otherwise. A DLT platform allows central banks and market participants to monitor transactions on a shared and transparent platform. DLT platforms provide several benefits such as improved privacy, transaction security for tracking and verification as well as process automation via smart contracts without the need for a trusted intermediary. An example would be foreign remittances, whereby currencies are transferred from an account to another across different economies and possibly different platforms. Smart contracts may be programmed with a high level of technical complexity to coordinate the transfer of currency between different platforms. Such efficiency gains can lead to lower transaction costs, thus reducing a key barrier for many financially excluded to use formal financial products or services.

The Architecture box refers to the legal claims structure based on the operational role for the central bank. An extended discussion of this subject matter will be presented in Chapter 3 of this report.

From the perspective of another framework, Scorer (2017) identifies eight technology requirements when designing a CBDC. These requirements are summarized below:

(i) **Resilience:** CBDCs should be expected to operate 24 hours a day for 365 days a year. This is high operational resilience of 99.999% availability with a limited downtime of about 5 minutes a year.

(ii) **Security:** CBDCs need to be secure against cyberattacks, such as unauthorized access to data that would disrupt the CBDC operation (for example, distributed denial-of-service attacks, hacking, phishing, ransomware, malware).

(iii) **Scalability:** CBDCs may replace existing fiat currency, therefore, CBDCs need to scale upwards to process several thousand transactions per second.

(iv) **Transaction processing:** CBDCs need to provide settlement finality, that is, near-instantaneous or real-time settlement. This would be useful for settlements between retail payments to the central banks, where it can be completed almost instantly in real-time.

(v)   **Confidentiality:** CBDC users should be able to transact privately, where transaction details are only visible to the counterparties of that transaction; however, this does not mean anonymously, as central banks should be able to identify and relate these transactions to real-world identities to prevent any money laundering activities or funding of terrorism activities.

(vi) **Interoperability:** To facilitate cross-economy CBDC systems, every CBDC system needs to be able to operate between various CBDC systems. This would promote faster foreign remittances and improve transaction settlement time and fees.

(vii) **Innovation:** With the use of smart contracts, CBDCs could enable the overlay of innovative features and services such as automated annual tax returns, automated tracking, and payments of goods and services linked to an individual.

(viii) **Future proofing:** As technology evolves, CBDCs need to be able to upgrade without impacting daily operations. One future development is the use of quantum computing.

Potential Pros and Cons of a Central Bank Digital Currency

The goals of governments exploring or implementing CBDCs tend to focus on a variety of issues based on the notion that centralized digital currencies provide greater visibility of economic activity and enhance the ability of central banks to monitor and influence the finance sector through targeted interventions. Among prominent goals or priorities, central banks see potential benefits of implementing CBDCs as including: greater financial inclusion, access to payments, and payment efficiency and resilience; greater ability to combat money laundering and the financing of terrorism; monetary sovereignty over the growing use of alternative digital currencies; and increased competition within an economy's payments sector (Soderberg et al. 2022).

Research has suggested that CBDCs have the potential to increase gross domestic product by as much as 3 percentage points, as a result of reductions in real interest rates, distortionary taxes, and monetary transaction costs (Barrdear and Kumhof 2016). A case for reduced costs is also commonly made by proponents of CBDCs, especially for cross-border payments. The prototype platform of multiple CBDCs developed by the Bank for International Settlements Innovation Hub discussed earlier in this report found that international transfers and foreign exchange operations could be done more efficiently than traditional cross-border transfers and reduce cost to users by as much as half (BIS 2021a).

Time will tell how effectively CBDCs achieve such outcomes, however, more broadly, the interest of governments in CBDCs appears to stem largely from the risks associated with growing consumer demand for cryptocurrencies, including stablecoins such as Tether, USD Coin, DAI, and others (Sier 2022, Kapronasia 2022). Driven primarily by the growth of DLT and higher digital investment from venture capital, the global cryptocurrency market is projected to grow from $910.3 million in 2021 to more than $1.9 billion by 2028 (Fortune Business Insights 2022). Cryptocurrencies are notoriously volatile, loosely regulated, and have the potential to undermine broader financial stability.

With CBDCs, governments may see an opportunity to satisfy demand for digital currencies while maintaining the ability to implement monetary policies to control growth, manage inflation, and ensure financial stability.

As the excitement behind CBDCs continues to propel central banks to explore this innovation, criticism is also growing out of fear of their potentially negative impacts. Some of the most common perceived drawbacks of CBDCs include giving central banks too much control of the currency and making it possible for them to put restrictions on the types of transactions allowed, potential privacy issues because CBDCs will give central banks data on every transaction, or limitations in uptake (especially in developing economies) with many people unable to access the necessary technology or lacking digital skills to use a digital currency effectively. There is also concern about the potential for account-based, directly-issued CBDCs to position central banks in direct competition with commercial banks. With commercial banks competing for deposits, CBDCs may destabilize the commercial banking sector and trigger bank solvency and liquidity issues (ING 2020).

As more economies pursue CBDCs, the understanding of their advantages and disadvantages over fiat and alternative digital currencies will become more apparent. At this stage, it is clear that more research is needed to fully comprehend the impact of CBDCs, and how these effects will differ between economies depending on local circumstances and needs.

Central Bank Digital Currencies in Asia–Pacific Economic Cooperation Member Economies

Most of APEC's member economies have at least begun studying the potential of CBDCs, with a few already conducting pilot studies. Several international collaboration projects involving APEC member economies are also under way (e.g., mCBDC Bridge and Project Dunbar). To better understand the status of CBDCs within APEC economies, ADB, with support of the APEC Secretariat, issued a survey to members of the APEC Finance Ministers' Process.

Thirteen APEC member economies[4] responded to the survey, which was designed to gather information on how different economies viewed CBDCs as a potential driver for financial inclusion. The results of the survey are summarized below.

Status of Central Bank Digital Currency Development

Most respondents noted that their economies were currently conducting CBDC research, with only a relative few having progressed to the piloting stage. In the type of CBDC explored, half of the respondents were intending to implement either solely retail or a combined retail and wholesale CBDC (Figure 5).

---

[4] APEC economies responding to the survey included Australia; Brunei Darussalam; Canada; Hong Kong, China; Japan; Malaysia; Mexico; the Philippines; the Russian Federation; Taipei,China; Thailand; the United States; and Viet Nam.

Figure 5: Status and Type of Central Bank Digital Currency Being Developed in Select Asia–Pacific Economic Cooperation Economies

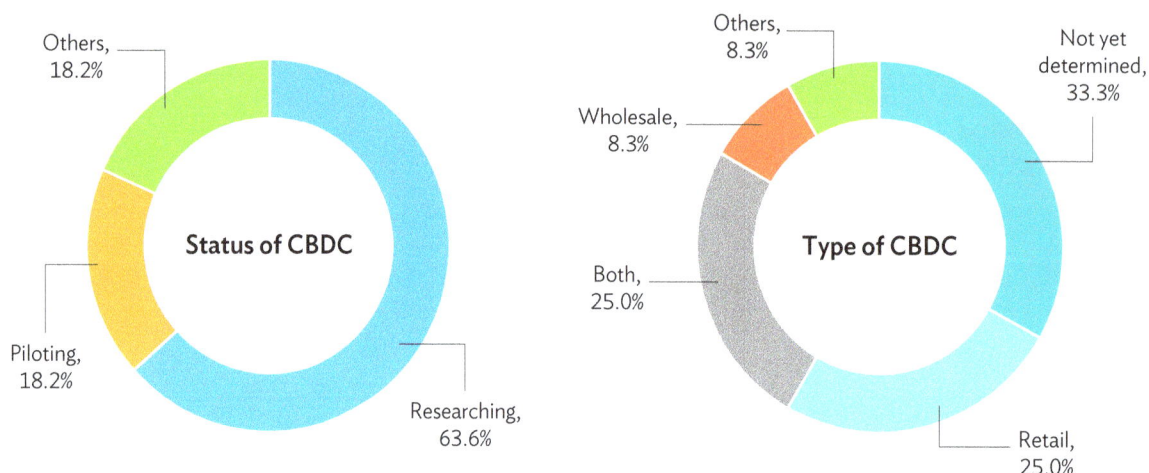

Others, 18.2%

Piloting, 18.2%

Researching, 63.6%

Status of CBDC

Others, 8.3%

Wholesale, 8.3%

Both, 25.0%

Not yet determined, 33.3%

Retail, 25.0%

Type of CBDC

CBDC = central bank digital currency.
Source: Authors.

Perceived Gains from a Central Bank Digital Currency

Views on the benefits to the finance sector to be gained through a CBDC differed between economies (Figure 6). Many of these differences were evident between developed economies (i.e., members of the Group of 20 [G20]) and developing economies (non-G20 economies). The largest share of respondents answered "*spurring innovation for payment systems*" as a high benefit of a CBDC. This perception is especially strong among non-G20 economies. Similarly, a higher share of non-G20 economies (than G20 economies) identified "*realizing safer, faster, and cheaper cross-border payment system*" is a high benefit of CBDCs. By contrast, while a majority of the G20 economy respondents believed "*extending public access to safe central bank money*" to be a high benefit of a CBDC, majority of non-G20 economies did not share this view (Figure 7). Lastly, enhancing financial inclusion was not perceived to be a strong benefit of CBDCs by all participating economies. Interestingly, some economies perceived that a CBDC would improve equity securities settlement (i.e., a safer, faster, and cheaper means of executing transactions) and transaction tracing to monitor illegal transactions.

Figure 6: Perceived Benefits of a Central Bank Digital Currency

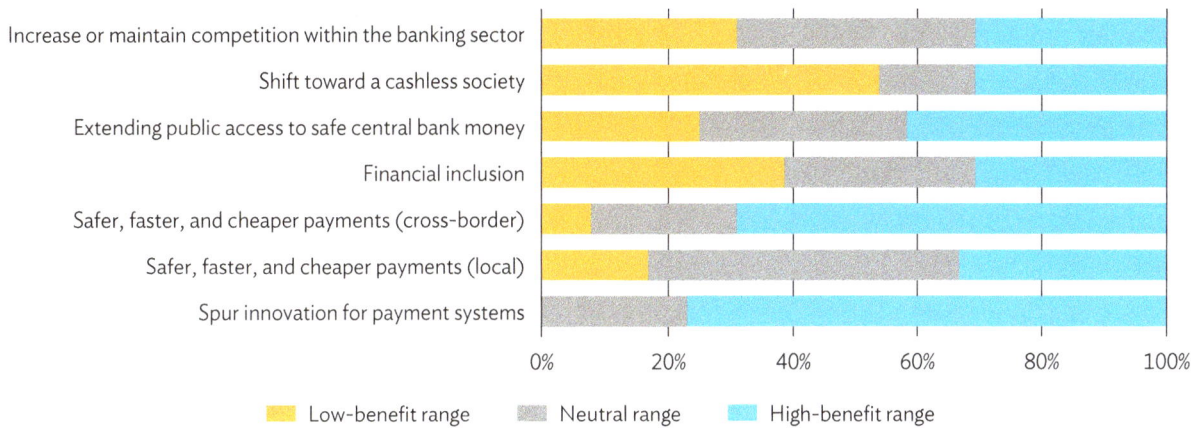

| | Low-benefit range | Neutral range | High-benefit range |

Source: Authors.

Figure 7: Perceived Benefits of a Central Bank Digital Currency, Non-G20 Economies

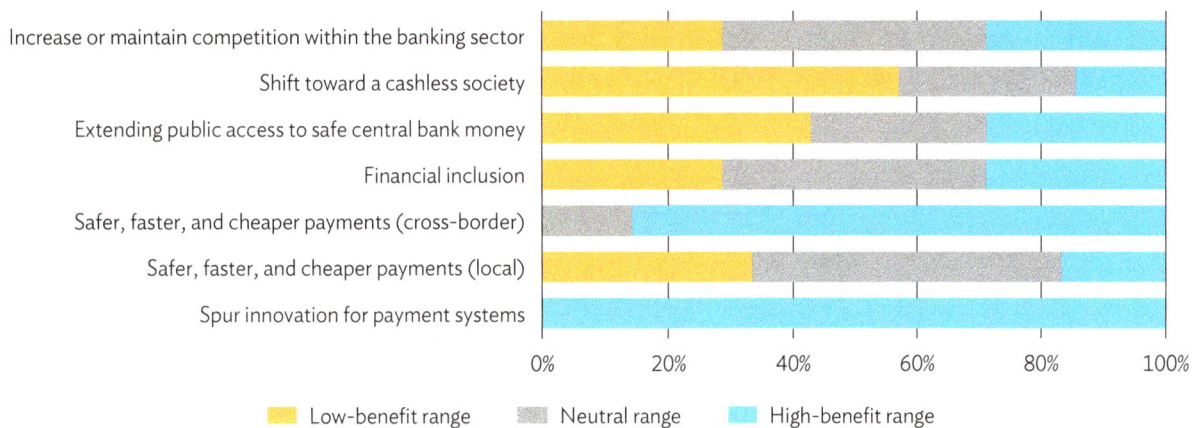

| | Low-benefit range | Neutral range | High-benefit range |

G20 = Group of 20.
Source: Authors.

Perceived Risks of Central Bank Digital Currencies

The survey revealed that non-G20 economy respondents rated potential risks of a CBDC higher than G20 economies, especially on "*cybersecurity*" and "*privacy*". By contrast, none of the identified risks are perceived to be a primary risk by G20 economies. Interestingly, one economy pointed to the high operational burden to the central bank as a major risk (Figures 8 and 9).

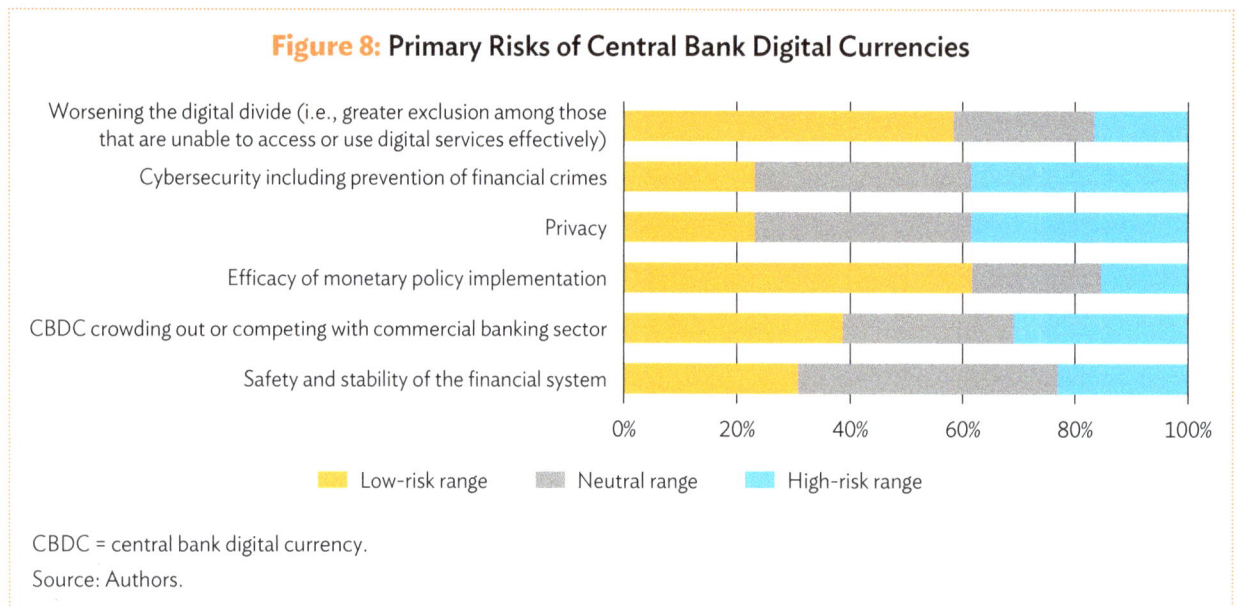

Figure 8: Primary Risks of Central Bank Digital Currencies

CBDC = central bank digital currency.
Source: Authors.

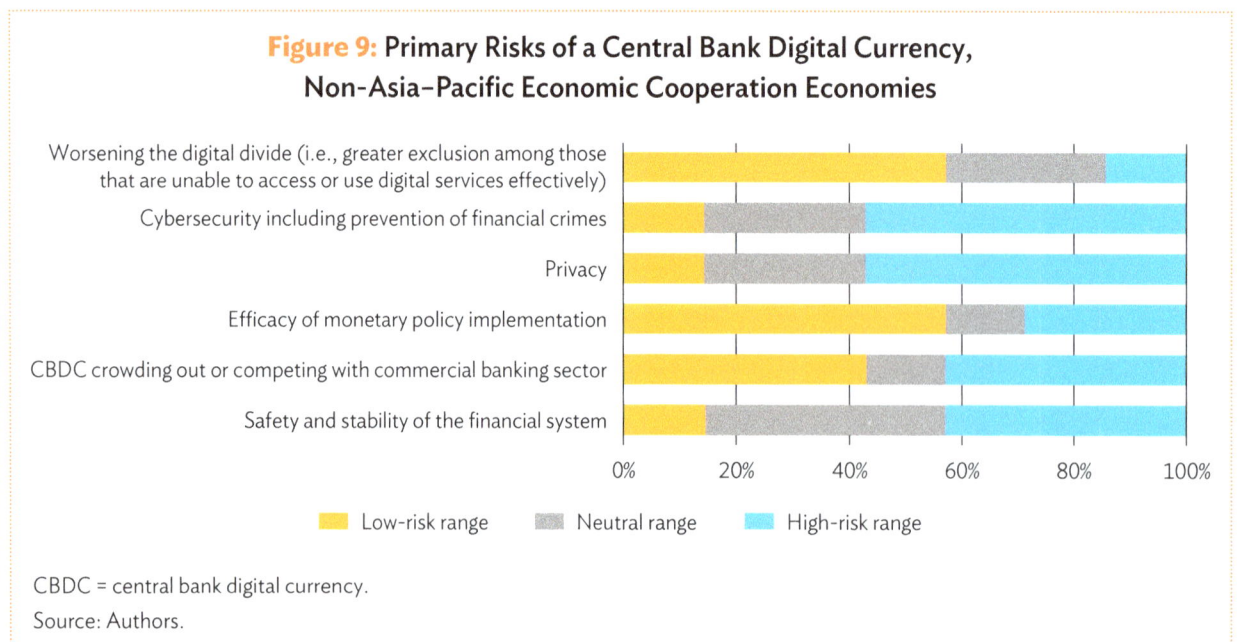

Figure 9: Primary Risks of a Central Bank Digital Currency,
Non–Asia–Pacific Economic Cooperation Economies

CBDC = central bank digital currency.
Source: Authors.

Perceptions of Central Bank Digital Currencies as a Potential Driver of Financial Inclusion

While the majority of respondent economies did not believe CBDCs could enhance financial inclusion, if a CBDC was to drive such inclusion, the majority of the participating economies identified that the reduced cost of transactions would be the primary driver (Figures 10 and 11).

Figure 10: Perceived Value of a Central Bank Digital Currency as a Potential Driver of Financial Inclusion

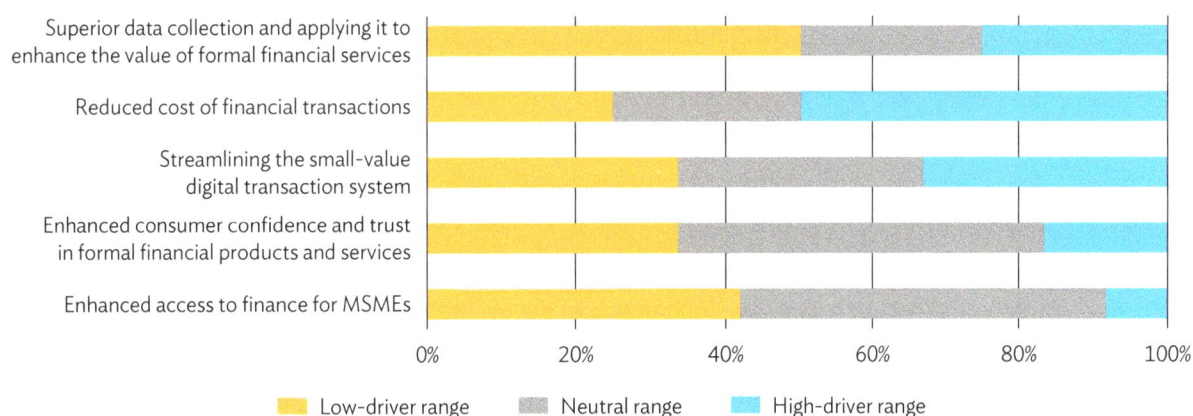

MSMEs = micro, small, and medium-sized enterprises.
Source: Authors.

Figure 11: Perceived Value of a Central Bank Digital Currency as a Potential Driver of Financial Inclusion, Non-G20 Economies

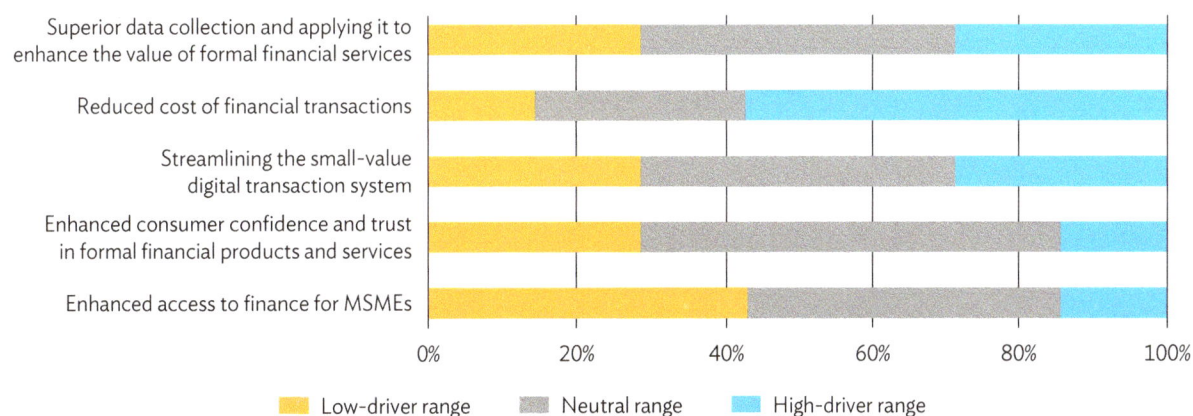

G20 = Group of 20, MSMEs = micro, small, and medium-sized enterprises.
Source: Authors.

Perceived Challenges of Implementing a Central Bank Digital Currency for Enhancing Financial Inclusion

The perceived challenges of implementing a CBDC for greater financial inclusion underlines some of the important reasons respondents did not view CBDCs as an effective way to improve financial inclusion. For example, many respondents said their economies already have highly advanced digitalization of payment systems (especially in retail transactions). As such, enhancing financial inclusion is often not a primary aim of a potential CBDC. However, respondents said that obstacles to a CBDC enhancing financial inclusion were primarily related to limited digital and financial literacy and infrastructure. Literacy issues included awareness of safe use of digital financial services and how to save and plan a financial budget, etc. Infrastructure needs included availability of a safe and robust payment and financial ecosystem and infrastructure gaps between rural and urban areas.

Potential Strategies to Incentivize Society to Use Central Bank Digital Currency

Most respondents did not give examples of how they might offer specific incentives to support adoption of a CBDC across society. Most respondents shared a belief that if the CBDC is proven to be secure and offers valuable features such as a low-cost means of payments, then it will be accepted by society. However, respondents in one economy pointed out that its industry partners were incentivized by the opportunity for first-hand learning from the CBDC project led by their respective central bank.

Useful Support to Accelerate the Progress of Central Bank Digital Currency Development

Respondents pointed out the need for cooperation among central banks and the value of assistance from those economies that have already advanced CBDC development, including building technological and organizational capacity. Given the complexity of developing a CBDC, economies were aware of their limitations in effectively and efficiently building a CBDC alone. In addition, respondents highlighted the importance of engagement with and support from broad stakeholder groups (via public–private partnership schemes) to codevelop infrastructure and establish effective legal, governance, and risk protocols. Key stakeholders identified by respondents included financial authorities and institutions, nonbank payment system providers, information technology specialists, and legal experts.

Working with External Parties to Support the Development of a Central Bank Digital Currency

Several respondents reported that they were already collaborating with many stakeholders, including central banks from other economies, international organizations such as the International Monetary Fund and the BIS (and their affiliates), industry partners such as financial institutions (i.e., banks and nonbank money issuers), technology companies, law firms, and research institutes. Collaborations could include support to assess potential benefits, costs, and risks of a CBDC; jointly developing and facilitating a platform to pilot transactions (including cross-border systems); and leveraging the resources and expertise of third parties to support development.

2 Potential Role of Central Bank Digital Currencies: Opportunities and Challenges of Central Bank Digital Currencies for Financial Inclusion

Recognizing the positive effects of financial products and services on economic growth and development, many governments have prioritized financial inclusion as a key component of their development strategies. Over the past decade, access to financial products and services such as savings, credit, payments, insurance, or investment services has grown considerably across the Asia–Pacific region. However, despite much progress, significant populations remain unserved or underserved.

The emergence of digital technologies, supported by the proliferation of mobile phones and the emergence of digital platforms, is creating new opportunities for financial inclusion. Innovative fintech-enabled solutions are being introduced to enhance the value and viability of formal financial services and making it possible for millions of unbanked people to engage in the formal finance sector for the first time. Advantages of digital financial services such as lower transaction costs, greater convenience, or the potential for enhanced product design to better meet the needs of consumers have been identified as important opportunities to overcome traditional constraints hindering financial inclusion.

The role of digital finance in achieving financial inclusion gained greater attention recently as a result of the COVID-19 pandemic. As the crisis unfolded, it became apparent that governments which had already invested in developing strong digital infrastructure and actively promoted adoption of digital financial services were more capable of maintaining economic activity during lockdown periods (ADB 2021) and directly supporting vulnerable populations through government-to-person payments (Rutkowski et al. 2020). As governments digest the lessons of the pandemic and turn to post-pandemic recovery, they identify faster digital transformation as a core component in many of their strategies.

Exploring Opportunities of Central Bank Digital Currencies for Financial Inclusion

Well-designed CBDCs offer benefits to society and can improve financial inclusion. Many of the challenges in doing so are those that the private finance sector has been facing. These include building confidence and trust in digital financial services among consumers for whom they are new, facilitating a large volume of small-value transactions, and the total cost of transactions. This section explores opportunities to advance financial inclusion that CBDCs may enable.

Enhanced Access to Finance for Small Enterprises

The characteristics of CBDCs introduced in Chapter 1 can benefit micro, small, and medium-sized enterprises (MSMEs). For example, businesses can reduce the settlement cycle through the live transaction feature of CBDCs (Deloitte 2022). This improves the efficiency of cross-border trades. Conventionally, payments for such trade involve central and commercial banks in home and trade-partner economies and it thus takes time to settle the transaction (Soni 2022). This feature can also help MSMEs to better predict their cash flows.

Enhanced Consumer Confidence and Trust

A lack of trust in formal financial institutions, especially in digital financial services, is common among many unbanked or underbanked individuals who may be unwilling to access and use financial products and services. Central bank-issued digital currency, as opposed to digital financial services offered by private organizations (digital payments, mobile money, etc.) or decentralized cryptocurrencies, may prove more appealing among individuals and thus increase the demand for formal financial services. Many individuals "distrust" issuing agents and thus do not use private services, which supports this fact (Blumenstock et al. 2015, Nelms and Rea 2017). In cryptocurrencies, the volatile nature of their prices also compromise their potential as a means of storing savings/wealth. Further, private cryptocurrencies are often held and traded on exchanges (unregulated in most cases) and cases exist of cryptocurrency exchanges being hacked with funds stolen as a result of compromised security systems.[5]

CBDCs on the other hand will be direct liabilities of central banks and regulated by them. As mentioned in Chapter 1, the value of a CBDC against the fiat currency can be either constant or altered periodically based on the rate of inflation or the official cash rate. Bordo and Levin (2017) argue that bearing interest enhances the role of CBDCs as a "secure store of value," while the majority of central banks are studying noninterest-bearing CBDCs, as this introduces competition against conventional bank deposits. These features of CBDCs improve the trust of the users (i.e., individuals and MSMEs). Like cash and e-money payment instruments, there may be a risk of CBDCs being stolen. Often, such fraud is enabled by human error (Khiaonarong and Humphrey 2022) and when sensitive user information is stolen. A CBDC designed with an optional custodial feature may in principle help users with low digital and financial literacy to use this innovation in daily transactions more safely.

Streamlining the Small-Value Digital Transaction System

Building a new digital system to handle the high volume of small-value transactions may not be attractive for commercial banks or e-money operators to pursue (Didenko and Buckley 2021). However, to include various economic participants, this type of transaction needs to be facilitated. As Chapter 1 notes, retail CBDCs may be able to handle a large volume of small-value transactions. Streamlining the retail CBDC system will thus help improve financial inclusion.

---

[5]   For example, Mt. Gox in 2011–2014, Coincheck in 2018, and Ronin Network in 2022.

Reduced Cost of Financial Transactions

Conventional means of payment can be costly. For example, in storing money in a bank account and withdrawing cash to shop at a retailer, there can be at least two types of costs: an account holding fee and a withdrawal fee. Even for digital transactions, transaction fees are often applied. In addition, transactions that involve a direct money transfer between bank accounts (e.g., between consumers) would also be subject to transaction fees. Some governments and central banks are developing fast and low-cost transaction systems.[6] However, these single-economy systems may not resolve issues relating to cross-border payment costs. CBDCs may be able to substantially reduce these international-related transaction costs (Khiaonarong and Humphrey 2022, J.P. Morgan 2021). The World Bank (2021) estimates that international remittances cost 6% (for a $200 transaction) on average in 2021. According to J.P. Morgan (2021), multi-economy CBDCs can save $100 billion in remittance fees each year. The cost of banking has been a main reason people choose to be unbanked/underbanked (BSP 2019). CBDCs can therefore encourage these financially excluded clusters of society to access the formal financial system.

Superior Data Collection and Applying It to Enhance the Value of Formal Financial Services

Supported by fintech tools, financial service providers are collecting large volumes of consumer data, and these are utilized to offer more tailored products and services to their clients. This can help address a root cause of financial exclusion by creating a better value proposition for the unbanked or underserved and increasing demand for formal financial products and services. However, as enhancing the value of their products and services (and strengthening the business case) are the primary focus of the financial institutions, financial exclusion may be better addressed by the central banks by using the data on individuals collected through the use of CBDCs.

Governments (and researchers) can study this data to gain more in-depth understanding of various consumer segments, including behaviors, needs, and vulnerabilities (e.g., Auer et al. 2021). This could give governments the ability to enhance their social welfare interventions, including government-to-person payments, a proven valuable use case for bringing the unbanked into the formal financial system. Using the data collected through CBDCs, governments could potentially not only enhance the efficiencies of government-to-person payments, but also direct targeted interventions supporting the base of the economy with far more accuracy and impact. Related to this, Davoodalhosseini (2021) argues that CBDCs can improve the effectiveness of a monetary stimulus that injects funds directly to the target (so called "helicopter drops").

---

[6]   Indonesia recently introduced a real-time 24/7 payment system called BI-FAST. According to Bank Indonesia (2021), the cost of each transaction to customers is limited to Rp2,500 (about $0.17). For a micropayment, this cost can be a few percent of the transaction.

Enhanced Efficiencies

CBDCs can also improve the efficiency of transactions. Project Hamilton (a joint initiative of the Federal Reserve Bank of Boston and Massachusetts Institute of Technology), in its first phase study, has shown that CBDCs can handle up to 1.7 million transactions per second. Considering that VISA, one of the major electronic funds transfers services in the world, can handle 65,000 transactions per second (Fonda 2022), CBDCs may be able to handle a considerably larger volume of micropayments.

In addition, within a multi-CBDCs platform, a number of different CBDCs issued by participating central banks can be connected within a global system (Chapter 1). Residents of a participating economy can make international transactions using their own economy's CBDC to minimize or eliminate remittance costs. This makes the facilitation of cross-border transactions easier, lowers costs, and enhances financial inclusion.

Challenges of Central Bank Digital Currencies for Financial Inclusion

While CBDCs may offer opportunities for financial inclusion, as noted, they also represent unique challenges for policy makers in introducing the innovation with the expectation that they will have a positive effect on financial inclusion. This is especially the case in emerging markets. As Bull et al. (2021) point out, as a digital financial service, a CBDC faces all of the same challenges that banks and fintechs currently struggle with to make such services accessible and viable for the unbanked or underbanked. Common constraints hindering the impact on financial inclusion, particularly among those at the base of the economy, include inadequate or unreliable infrastructure to enable digital financial services (including mobile phone or internet connections), lack of access to required hardware (e.g., phones, computers, etc.), limited digital literacy or capabilities, or lack of awareness of digital alternatives and their benefits (UNESCAP 2022, Hunter and Taylor 2020). These issues are typically exacerbated among women, who also make up the majority of the financially excluded.

Another important constraint limiting the viability of a CBDC to enhance financial inclusion in emerging markets is the current reliance among the unbanked or underserved on the traditional cash economy. Even if access to digital financial services, including a CBDC, is provided, adequate opportunities to spend digital currency, or at least cash out with ease, remains a critical necessity in many emerging markets. Much work is still needed to change the behaviors of low-income consumers to successfully alter their preferences from cash to any form of digital currency.

Moving beyond these general demand-side challenges, the opportunities of CBDCs can also be viewed as a double-edged sword, leading to potential negative impacts on the broader financial system. Some of these issues are explored as follows.

Impact on Financial Stability

Centrals banks have long been the lender of last resort to maintain the stability of their respective financial systems. However, by issuing a CBDC, some are concerned that the central bank may cause financial instability. The former president of the Deutsche Bundesbank, Jens Weidmann, points out that CBDCs may induce bank runs in a crisis (Deutsche Bundesbank 2019, Pinsent Masons 2018). This is because, in such a time, investors and individuals may be more inclined to convert their assets into highly liquid CBDCs, and in the digital world such conversion can be done almost instantly through mobile phones or computers. A stable financial system is a crucial condition for any financial inclusion measure to be effective. While this may only become an issue in economic downturns, it would need to be considered at the design phase of a CBDC.

Potential "Competition" with Other Fiat Currencies

As Kiff et al. (2020) argue, CBDCs of reserve currency economies may become a substitution for local fiat currencies issued by other economies as cross-border transactions may be settled more efficiently (e.g., in remittance cost and time). This then is likely to increase financial instability in those economies (Edwards 2021) and may reduce local authorities' ability to conduct monetary policy (IMF 2020).

Potential "Competition" with the Conventional Finance Sector

Further, as indicated by the benefits of CBDCs, such digital currencies may compete against products and services currently offered by conventional financial institutions. As the finance sector plays an important role in the economy and society, this type of competition may crowd out and distort the financial system, and therefore, reduce overall stability. As such, the benefits and opportunities of CBDCs may be a double-edged sword. Policy makers thus should communicate with the finance sector in deciding to introduce CBDCs. The two-tier system discussed in the next chapter is a suggested solution.

3 Connecting Central Bank Digital Currencies with the Existing Financial System to Improve Financial Inclusion

CBDCs can connect to their respective economies and the global financial system through several pathways. CBDCs can be designed as a digital alternative to cash and can be integrated with the existing financial system as a widely accepted medium of exchange and a store of value. Similar to cash and bank deposits, a CBDC can be a legal form of money, used in any economy, and would allow conversion from an economy's currency to another.

A CBDC can also be designed to offer claims directly to individual clients or indirectly via authorized intermediaries. In either case, central banks would be responsible for the issuance of digital currency and the management of these accounts. If a CBDC is to have a meaningful impact on advancing financial inclusion, there are a number of important considerations in how the CBDC is integrated into the existing financial system.

Direct versus Indirect Central Bank Digital Currency Systems

Auer and Böhme (2020a) point out that when designing a CBDC, it is important to consider the key roles it serves in facilitating access to the CBDC itself (Figure 12).

A CBDC system could be one-tier (direct CBDC), whereby the central bank is responsible for all aspects of the system including issuance of digital currency and managing retail payments, including the verification of transactions and the maintenance of accounts. This model assumes it is operated by the central bank only and no intermediaries are involved. The central bank is responsible for the payment system's reliability, speed, and efficiency. In this model, the central bank onboards all accounts, including identification and all relevant documents in compliance with know-your-customer (KYC) regulation. This model is an unlikely scenario given the large and significant number of accounts that the central bank would have to manage, operate, and monitor.

In a two-tier CBDC system (indirect CBDC), the central bank acts as a "platform" and develops the technology to issue the CBDC to authorized intermediaries who, in turn, are responsible for dealing with all customer-related transactions. The two-tier CBDC system can potentially work alongside the existing financial ecosystem, whereby the authorized intermediaries handle retail transactions with retail clients and settle wholesale accounts with central banks. In this system, the central bank only keeps records of wholesale holdings and is not involved in the record-keeping process of individual clients. Therefore, any dispute resolution or proof of claim will have to be processed by authorized intermediaries.

In addition to direct and indirect CBDCs, Auer and Böhme (2020a) envision a third system—a possible two-tier CBDC system (hybrid CBDC) where a group of payment service providers acts as authorized intermediaries and provides the option for the central bank to switch between them in the event of system malfunction. This allows the system to continue to operate if a retail bank system is being undermined. Other advantages include offering a more resilient system than direct or indirect CBDC options. However, this may cost more to set up and operate in the long run. The authorized intermediaries would have to allow the central bank to access all retail accounts, therefore, a distributed copy of retail client accounts would need to be accessible from other intermediaries as well as the central banks in this system.

Figure 12: Overview of Potential Retail Central Bank Digital Currency Architecture

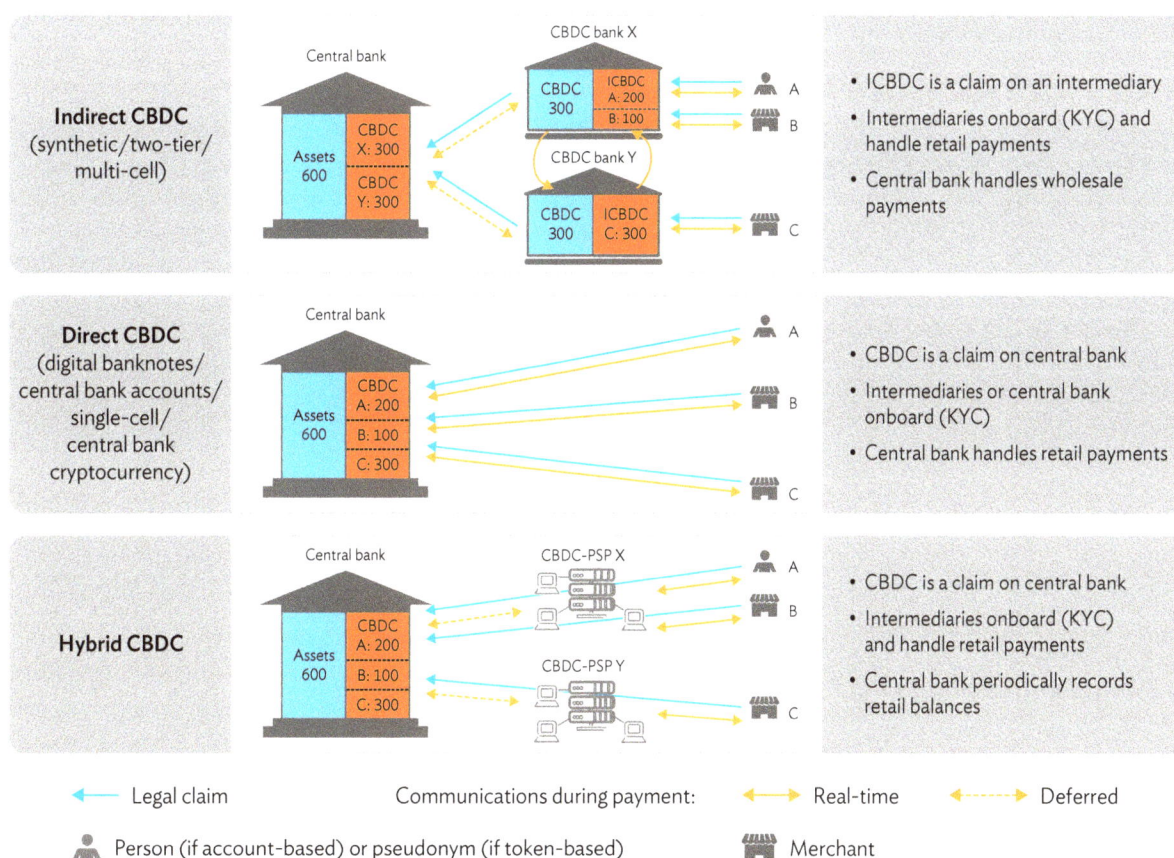

CBDC = central bank digital currency, ICBDC = indirect central bank digital currency, KYC = know-your-customer, PSP = payment service provider.

Notes: In all three architectures, the CBDC is issued only by the central bank. In the indirect CBDC architecture (top panel), this is done indirectly, and an ICBDC in the hands of consumers represents a claim on an intermediary. In the other two architectures, consumers have a direct claim on the central bank. In the direct CBDC model (center panel), the central bank handles all payments in real time and thus keeps a record of all retail holdings. The hybrid CBDC model (bottom panel) is an intermediate solution providing for direct claims on the central bank while real-time payments are handled by intermediaries. In this architecture, the central bank retains a copy of all retail CBDC holdings, allowing it to transfer holdings from one payment service provider to another in the event of a technical failure. All three architectures allow for either account- or token-based access.

Source: Auer and Böhme (2020a).

Case Study 2: Thailand's Retail Central Bank Digital Currency Design Process

In Thailand, close to 70 million IDs have been registered to the country's real-time retail payment system known as PromptPay, which facilitates B114 billion (about $3.28 billion) in transactions per day. Despite the success of the platform, 45% of the population remains underbanked, without any basic financial products other than a bank account. The Bank of Thailand (BOT) recognizes the potential of a retail central bank digital currency (CBDC) as a possible solution for expanding access and adoption of formal financial products and services.

Since 2020, the BOT has been examining how a retail CBDC might be developed and deployed to achieve this goal. The CBDC, as a digital form of central bank money, should serve as an open and inclusive financial infrastructure for all players, including banks, nonbank payment service providers, and corporates. Key considerations include the integration of the potential CBDC with business platforms to achieve invoice tokenization and conditional payments, and how programmability features could enable new and innovative services for the general public. As a next step, the BOT plans to launch a small-scale live CBDC pilot in late 2022 until mid-2023.

As part of ongoing efforts, the BOT is cooperating with the private sector to investigate and determine the best design features of the CBDC. The central bank's role will be to ensure the resiliency and security of the system and set rules and standards around the CBDC. On the other hand, the private sector is expected to contribute to identifying use cases and benefits of the CBDC beyond the existing system. For example, a recently launched CBDC Hackathon by the BOT invites applicants to present and uncover innovative use cases as part of the innovation track of the CBDC pilot.

Further, the BOT has prioritized building awareness of the CBDC as well as digital financial literacy among the public. Such efforts include creating easy-to-digest infographics and communication campaigns via the BOT's social media channels, participating in television and podcast interviews, and hosting online webinars with educational institutions.

Source: Authors.

Key Components of Central Bank Digital Currency Design to Enable Financial Inclusion

Digital ID

A critical component for any form of digital currency to be successful is the ability to establish the true identity of the person transacting. Digital ID aims to do this for a range of online services. This is particularly useful for a CBDC, as it would allow central banks to manage KYC processes and execute transactions accurately and efficiently.

As noted by the United Nations Development Programme (UNDP 2019), a carefully designed digital ID system extends the benefits of financial inclusion to more people in the economy and allows essential interactions to be facilitated between consumers, companies, and government bodies. Digital ID needs to be created and used with individual consent, with the possibility of remote verification processes and at low cost, while maintaining data privacy and promoting trust in its usage.

When digital ID is implemented, it has the potential to save time in verifying the identity of individuals and could be linked directly to a digital wallet, granted the quality of the information technology (IT) infrastructure is adequate. The digital wallet would be useful when transacting online, such as booking an international flight or transferring money to another individual(s). Financial intermediaries can also benefit from the digital ID infrastructure as it is secure, efficient, and reduces fraud when onboarding individuals via the KYC process into the future digital ecosystem.

A fully functional and reliable digital ID system can have a significant impact on financial inclusion by enabling every individual in the economy to open a bank account, including those in rural and remote areas. Other benefits would include reducing tax fraud and identity theft through the unification of tax, medical, and/or healthcare information; education; voting and/or electoral services; and superannuation and/or pension fund information. A number of economies have already implemented their versions of a digital ID system, including Australia (myGovID), the Philippines (PhilSys ID), Singapore (SingPass), and others.

Payment Systems

Another important consideration is the potential for connecting a new CBDC to an existing payment system. The People's Bank of China began piloting the e-CNY (digital yuan) in April 2020 across four major cities and has gradually expanded to other cities. The central bank showcased the ease of using e-CNY during the 2022 Winter Olympics, with more than $315,000 e-CNY payments made daily and a growing pool of 261 million users by the end of 2021 (Jones 2022). Behind the scenes, the technologies connected the retail and wholesale banking systems, which has allowed users to sign up for an account using their mobile phone number on their smartphone. At the time of writing, no economy-wide rollout date was set. However, future plans include collaboration with the BIS on its mBridge project to expand e-CNY functionality with other economies such as Hong Kong, China; Thailand; and the United Arab Emirates.

Interoperability

A potential feature of CBDCs that could have a significant impact on financial inclusion is the integration of multiple CBDC systems to provide interoperability between different economies and currencies. A CBDC with higher interoperability might lead to better adoption and success. However, achieving this would require a great deal of cooperation between economies and trading partners to develop a CBDC system that is compatible with each other. This would include establishing operating and technical standards in the payment systems, security in encryption and decryption of transactions across multiple CBDC systems, and consideration of shared commonalities in payment settlement infrastructure and regulatory authorities.

Interoperability would greatly facilitate cross-border payments and significantly reduce cross-currency exchange rate risk. This would lead to greater efficiency in the payment systems and lower transaction costs, benefiting lower socioeconomic groups. Lower transaction costs and open access to all citizens, enabled through a digital ID scheme, would in turn support the inclusion of individuals previously underserved or unbanked in the economy.

Auer et al. (2021) extends the discussion of linking multiple CBDC systems, whereby the operations of CBDCs are based on common international and/or regional standards, by pointing out the importance of developing a shared technical interface and clearing processes. Linking multiple CBDC systems could involve economies governed by different laws and regulations (Figure 13), highlighting the need for close cooperation and consultation between economies to ensure frictions and barriers are reduced to enhance CBDC interoperability.

Figure 13: Multiple Central Bank Digital Currency Arrangements Based on Linking Multiple Central Bank Digital Currency Systems

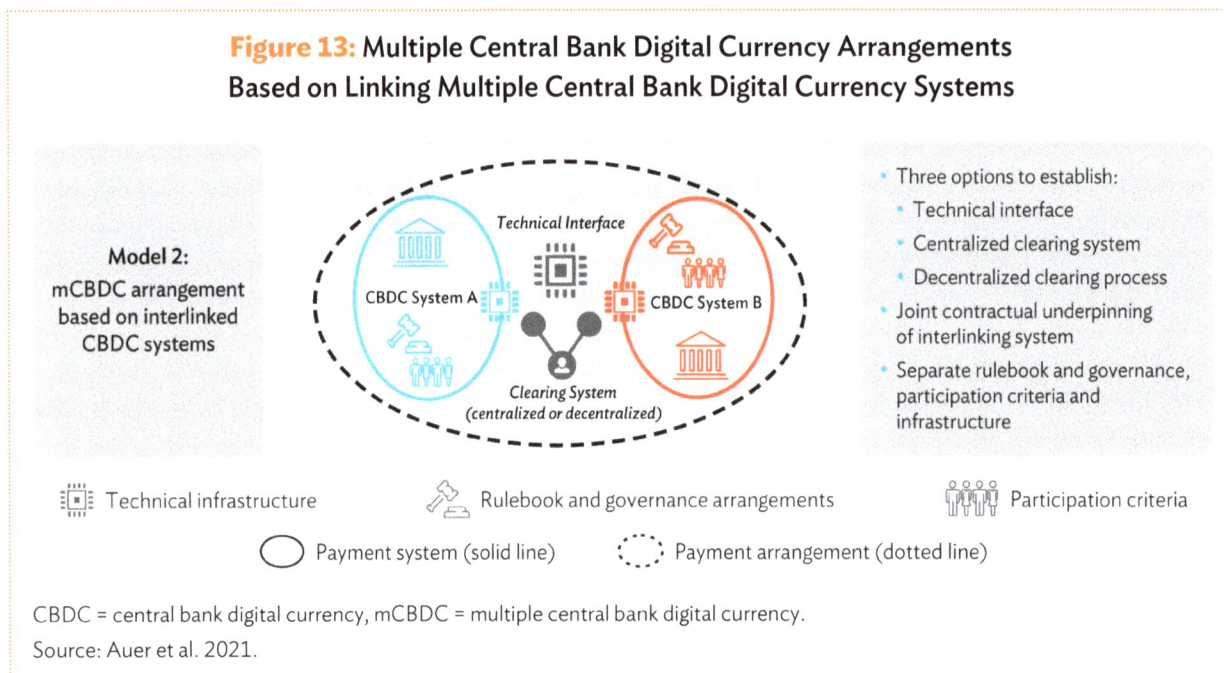

Model 2: mCBDC arrangement based on interlinked CBDC systems

Technical Interface

CBDC System A

CBDC System B

Clearing System (centralized or decentralized)

- Three options to establish:
  - Technical interface
  - Centralized clearing system
  - Decentralized clearing process
- Joint contractual underpinning of interlinking system
- Separate rulebook and governance, participation criteria and infrastructure

Technical infrastructure   Rulebook and governance arrangements   Participation criteria

Payment system (solid line)   Payment arrangement (dotted line)

CBDC = central bank digital currency, mCBDC = multiple central bank digital currency.
Source: Auer et al. 2021.

Strategies to Incentivize Society to Embrace Central Bank Digital Currencies

A number of strategies can be developed to promote and incentivize the take-up of CBDCs. First, a market-based perspective suggests that CBDCs will flourish and the general public will actively use them if they deliver cost savings to end-users. The benefits of lower transaction costs with CBDCs (than fiat currency) will underpin natural demand for the innovative currency versus current alternative forms of payments and settlement.

Second, the central bank and/or commercial banks (depending on the design of the CBDC) may offer the set-up of this new type of "digital bank account or ID" as a free service. To extend this, an economy's registrar of births, deaths, marriages, and divorce could implement an economy-wide ID scheme, whereby every new birth could have a digital ID to track medical history and education background. Subsequently, an economy-wide ID scheme could be used to provide grants, subsidies, relief payments, and/or expand for other payment purposes such as a CBDC.

Third, governments can incentivize the use of CBDCs by allowing it as a valid form of payment for various government services (e.g., government rates payments, land tax/levies, motor vehicle registration fees, etc.). An environment in which the government receives revenues from the general public as CBDCs will promote and incentivize increased use of CBDCs in everyday life.

Finally, with the programmability features of CBDCs, uptake could be driven through specific benefits designed for particular end-user groups. For example, this method could be especially effective in the government provision of subsidies for various economic programs. Governments can mandate that the subsidies can only be used via CBDC systems, thereby increasing the user adoption rate.

Case Study 3: The People's Republic of China's Programmed Central Bank Digital Currency to Support Low-Income Groups

The programmability of a central bank digital currency (CBDC) and smart contract design are attractive features for central banks to consider during the initial design phase. The People's Bank of China has been actively exploring the benefit of passing on government subsidies to facilitate a better fiscal and monetary implementation through its CBDC, known as the digital yuan or e-CNY. This is facilitated by deploying smart contracts for more complex payment functions such as conditional payments designed to influence economic activities by setting certain requirements as a precondition for payment. This type of programmability could potentially help drive financial inclusion and sustainability innovations among micro, small, and medium-sized enterprises, e.g., rural farmers, as demonstrated through several pilot programs utilizing the e-CNY.

In January 2022, the Pudong area of Shanghai issued the first e-CNY employment subsidy to individuals with employment difficulties. The targeted subsidy funds were distributed as e-CNY and distributed through a smart contracts function. A closed-loop management approach was used to ensure an efficient and healthy subsidy ecosystem that maximized the value of subsidies to the individuals.

Later in June 2022, a commercial bank in Jiangsu launched an e-CNY rural product called *yuanmengbao* which was specially tailored for Suzhou's new agricultural operators and farmers' operators. This innovative product has the advantages of rapid approval, simple materials and flexible guarantee methods, and the maximum amount can reach CNY2 million. Loans are issued to farmers' e-wallets as e-CNY, and can be linked to the farmers' "card type" hard wallets in the form of e-CNY.

Finally, in July 2022, the Fuyang district of Hangzhou implemented the subsidy fund for commercial organic fertilizer promotion supporting projects through e-CNY. Through this program, local farmers were invited to open an e-CNY account, after which the district agriculture and rural bureau and the district finance bureau would allocate the subsidy funds directly to the farmers' e-CNY wallet in the form of designated purposes. Following each successful transaction, the district agriculture and rural bureau conducts acceptances on the quantity of purchased commercial organic fertilizer.

As the People's Bank of China continues to experiment with the different applications of the e-CNY, early results from various pilot programs are demonstrating the potential of the CBDC to increase the efficiencies of government subsidies or other social welfare payments. Further, it is hoped that as the reach and applications of the e-CNY become more widespread, it will create a valuable use-case among traditionally unbanked or underbanked individuals or businesses and promote greater adoption of formal financial products and services.

Source: Authors.

4 Recommendations for Policy Makers and Regulators

As interest in CBDCs grows globally, findings from research and pilot programs will contribute to the collective understanding of the potential challenges and opportunities they represent. These findings will provide greater clarity on the impacts of a CBDC as a mechanism to enhance the reach and value of formal financial products and services to the unbanked. Based primarily on the experiences of the Asia-Pacific region, the following proposed actions intend to provide guidance to policy makers and regulators on ways they may prepare for and develop a CBDC that can be successful in achieving greater financial inclusion.

(i) Consider which design features of a CBDC will be most effective for financial inclusion

There is no one-size-fits-all model when it comes to CBDC design. Economies need to carefully consider what specific design features will result in the best financial inclusion gains in expanding access to formal financial products and services and enhancing the financial health of individuals or businesses through effective usage. Achieving this requires determining the key constraints for financial inclusion within the local economy and mapping these constraints to specific CBDC design features that can play a role in overcoming them. As part of this process, policy makers and regulators should consider the following:

- **Determine how CBDC design features would be recognized and impacted by current policies and regulations.** How an economy chooses to design its CBDC may result in various unforeseen policy or regulatory challenges which could have a significant impact on its viability to address financial inclusion. Certain design features, such as whether the CBDC is wholesale or retail, account-based or token-based, may be treated differently according to established legal frameworks. In the context of cross-border CBDC transactions, this issue also highlights the importance of assessing and standardizing regulatory and legal frameworks between economies.

- **Weigh the costs and benefits of a CBDC against other potential solutions in addressing financial inclusion.** While the prospect of implementing a CBDC to accelerate financial inclusion gains is appealing, it is important that governments and other stakeholders consider if it is indeed the most appropriate solution, or if this solution can complement already existing initiatives by central banks to advance financial inclusion. With new technology evolving at such a rapid pace, so too are opportunities to develop innovative solutions to address financial inclusion constraints. Implementing a CBDC is a significant challenge and requires high expertise, financial resources, and reliable infrastructure to operate effectively. Before committing to major investment, governments should consider the specific financial inclusion barriers most prominent in their economy and assess whether alternative technology solutions may actually be more effective or cost efficient.

■ **Pursue collaborations with other governments in the region to understand and address cross-border implications.** Joint assessments through cross-border collaborations can be a useful strategy to understand how a CBDC may be recognized in different jurisdictions. This may be especially important for transactions involving CBDCs to operate effectively between economies, including implications for international remittances. For example, high remittance receiving economies may need to consider regulatory reforms to address the potential for currency substitution when a CBDC is transferred from another economy and used in local markets.

(ii) **Prioritize addressing the required preconditions for successful digital financial inclusion**

As a digital product, a CBDC will encounter the same challenges currently experienced by service providers attempting to introduce digital financial services to the financially excluded. This includes persistent constraints such as limited trust in technology, reliance on the cash economy, or inadequate financial and digital literacy. These issues are exacerbated in developing economies, where many people may lack access to affordable or reliable infrastructure for participating in the digital economy, such as internet connectivity or even stable electricity networks. For a CBDC to be a viable solution for these disadvantaged groups, efforts must be made to create an environment where all consumers are both capable and comfortable using digital products and services. Examples of critical areas governments may need to consider for a CBDC to be a successful driver of financial inclusion include:

■ **Leverage the existing system of regulated financial intermediaries to distribute a CBDC and provide access channels.** Inclusion of nonbank service providers is especially important for meeting financial inclusion objectives, as it ensures access channels for those less connected with the formal financial system or the digital economy (i.e., those in remote areas). Use of existing networks can also support offline CBDC functionality critical for remote communities, which often have limited internet coverage or less reliable access to electricity.

■ **Address onerous identification and KYC requirements.** Identification requirements, especially for small transactions, are a critical barrier for financial inclusion. Integrating a CBDC with a domestic digital identification system, simplifying due diligence requirements through reforms, and promoting remote onboarding or e-KYC methods, such as tiered e-KYC based on transaction amounts, can strengthen a CBDC's impact on financial inclusion.

■ **Address financial and digital literacy and consumer protection needs.** Governments can play a major role in building awareness, skill levels, and trust in digital financial services through campaigns and public–private partnerships targeting disadvantaged segments of the population. Building trust in a CBDC will be of particular importance, as many segments of the population may resist moving beyond cash as the preferred medium of exchange. Society will need to have confidence not only in the CBDC, but also the technology systems used to facilitate it within the economy.

■ **Foster interoperability among multiple dimensions.** For a CBDC to become a viable currency option for all members of society, it will need to have broad adoption and integration throughout the economy. This requires ensuring interoperability across digital payment and settlement systems, including credit transfers, payment cards, and mobile money, as well as cross-border CBDC systems for international remittances. Data portability is also an important aspect of interoperability as it enables users to utilize their credit history to access other financial products and services.

(iii) **Recognize and manage the risks associated with introducing a CBDC**

A CBDC creates the unique prospect of putting digital central bank money in the hands of individuals and businesses, bringing new and potentially serious risks. One of the most significant risks associated with introducing a CBDC is the prospect of it directly competing against present day government-issued currencies, commercial banks, and the financial services sector, in general. The resulting impact on finance sector stability could have detrimental effects on financial inclusion. Examples of specific actions governments may need to take to ensure the safety and effectiveness of a CBDC include:

■ **Establish safeguards to mitigate the prospect of CBDCs crowding out or directly competing with the commercial banking sector and financial services industry.** Depending on how a CBDC is designed, its impact on banking and the finance sector can differ. Measures that could help reduce potentially negative impacts on finance sector stability include ensuring that a CBDC is not interest-bearing and implementing a two-tiered system for CBDC distribution. Conducting CBDC pilot programs and introducing the currency in a staged and progressive adoption plan can help better identify and understand potential risks and support the development of appropriate mitigation measures.

■ **Invest in enhancing cybersecurity technology and capabilities.** Every individual or business using a CBDC will be exposed to potential risks, including fraud, privacy breaches, human error, and others. Without adequate consumer protection policies and education programs (i.e., financial and digital literacy) in place to combat these issues, the perceived value of CBDC among potential users could be compromised. This issue may present a good opportunity for central banks to collaborate with the private sector to, for example, boost cybersecurity knowledge and capabilities or to undertake pilot programs with the aim of testing and reforming policy and regulatory frameworks as needed.

References

Asian Development Bank (ADB). 2021. *11th Asia-Pacific Financial Inclusion Forum: Emerging Priorities in the COVID-19 Era.* Manila.

Auer, R., and R. Böhme. 2020a. The Technology of Retail Central Bank Digital Currency. *BIS Quarterly Review.* BIS. https://www.bis.org/publ/qtrpdf/r_qt2003j.pdf.

———. 2020b. Central Bank Digital Currency: The Quest for Minimally Invasive Technology. *BIS Working Papers.* No. 948. Basel: BIS. https://www.bis.org/publ/work948.pdf.

Auer, R., J. Frost, L. Gambacorta, C. Monnet, T. Rice, and S.H. Shin. 2021. Central Bank Digital Currencies: Motives, Economic Implications and the Research Frontier. *BIS Working Papers.* No. 976. https://www.bis.org/publ/work976.pdf.

Bangko Sentral ng Pilipinas (BSP). 2019. *Financial Inclusion Survey.* https://www.bsp.gov.ph/Inclusive%20Finance/Financial%20Inclusion%20Reports%20and%20Publications/2019/2019FISToplineReport.pdf.

———. 2021. *Central Bank Digital Currency for the BSP: Fundamentals and Strategies.* https://www.bsp.gov.ph/Media_And_Research/Publications/CBDC_for_the_BSP_Book.pdf.

Bank for International Settlements (BIS). 2018. *Central Bank Digital Currencies.* Committee on Payments and Market Infrastructures – Markets Committee. March.

———. 2021a. *Inthanon-LionRock to mBridge: Building a Multi CBDC Platform for International Payments.* Basel: BIS. https://www.bis.org/publ/othp40.pdf.

———. 2021b. *CBDCs: An Opportunity for the Monetary System.* Basel: BIS. https://www.bis.org/publ/arpdf/ar2021e3.pdf.

BIS Innovation Hub. 2022. *International Settlements Using Multi-CBDCs.* https://www.bis.org/publ/othp47.pdf.

Bank of England. 2020. Central Bank Digital Currency Opportunities, Challenges and Design. *Discussion Paper.* London. March. https://www.bankofengland.co.uk/paper/2020/central-bank-digital-currency-opportunities-challenges-and-design-discussion-paper.

Bank Indonesia. 2021. Transformation of the Policy Mix and Acceleration of the Digital Economy and Finance. In *Economic Report of Indonesia 2021.* Jakarta. https://www.bi.go.id/en/publikasi/laporan/Documents/8_LPI2021_EN_Chapter_6.pdf#search=bi%2Dfast.

Bank of Thailand. 2021. *The Way Forward for Retail Central Bank Digital Currency in Thailand.* Bangkok. April. https://www.bot.or.th/Thai/DigitalCurrency/Documents/BOT_RetailCBDCPaper.pdf.

Barrdear, J., and M. Kumhof. 2016. The Macroeconomics of Central Bank Issued Digital Currencies. Bank of England. *Staff Working Paper.* No. 605. London.

Blumenstock, J.E., M. Callen, T. Ghani, and L. Koepke. 2015. Promises and Pitfalls of Mobile Money in Afghanistan: Evidence from a Randomized Control Trial. In Xin-She Yang, S. Sherratt, N. Dey, and A. Joshi, eds. *Proceedings of the Seventh International Conference on Information and Communication Technologies and Development*, pp. 1–10. London.

Board of Governors of the Federal Reserve System. 2022. *What is a Central Bank Digital Currency?* https://www.federalreserve.gov/faqs/what-is-a-central-bank-digital-currency.htm.

Bordo, D.M., and A.T. Levin. 2017. Central Bank Digital Currency and the Future of Monetary Policy. *NBER Working Paper Series.* No. 23711. Washington, DC: National Bureau of Economic Research. https://www.nber.org/system/files/working_papers/w23711/w23711.pdf.

Bull, G., W. Cook, M. Kerse, and S. Staschen. 2021. Is Financial Inclusion a Reason to Push Central Bank Digital Currencies? *Consultative Group to Assist the Poor (CGAP).* Blog. 14 May. https://www.cgap.org/blog/financial-inclusion-reason-push-central-bank-digital-currencies.

Cambridge. *Cambridge Bitcoin Electricity Consumption Index.* https://ccaf.io/cbeci/index (accessed 11 July 2022).

Chan, Aldar C-F. 2021. *UTXO in Digital Currencies: Account-Based or Token-Based? Or Both?* University of Hong Kong. https://arxiv.org/pdf/2109.09294.pdf.

Davoodalhosseini, M.S. 2021. Central Bank Digital Currency and Monetary Policy. *Journal of Economic Dynamics and Control.* 142. https://doi.org/10.1016/j.jedc.2021.104150.

Deloitte. 2020. *Are Central Bank Digital Currencies (CBDCs) the Money of Tomorrow?* https://www2.deloitte.com/content/dam/Deloitte/lu/Documents/financial-services/Banking/lu-are-central-bank-digital-currencies.pdf.

———. 2022. *Central Bank Digital Currencies: Building Block of the Future of Value Transfer.* https://www2.deloitte.com/content/dam/Deloitte/au/Documents/financial-services/deloitte-au-fsi-central-bank-digital-currencies-100322.pdf.

Demirgüç-Kunt, A., L. Klapper, D. Singer, and S. Ansar. 2022. *Global Findex Database 2021: Financial Inclusion, Digital Payments, and Resilience in the Age of COVID-19.* Washington, DC: World Bank. doi:10.1596/978-1-4648-1897-4.

Deutsche Bundesbank. 2019. *Jens Weidmann Sceptical about Central Bank Digital Currency.* https://www.bundesbank.de/en/tasks/topics/jens-weidmann-sceptical-about-central-bank-digital-currency-798326.

Didenko, N.A., and P.R. Buckley. 2021. *Central Bank Digital Currencies: A Potential Response to the Financial Inclusion Challenges of the Pacific.* Manila: Asian Development Bank. https://www.adb.org/publications/central-bank-digital-currencies-financial-inclusion-pacific.

Edwards, S. 2021. Central Bank Digital Currencies and the Emerging Markets: The Currency Substitution Challenge. *Challenge*. 64(5–6). pp. 413–424.

Federal Reserve Bank of Boston. 2022. *Project Hamilton Phase 1 Executive Summary*. 3 February. https://www.bostonfed.org/publications/one-time-pubs/project-hamilton-phase-1-executive-summary.aspx.

Fernandez-Villaverde, J., D. Sanches, L. Schillinge, and H. Uhlig. 2021. Central Bank Digital Currency: Central Banking for All? *Review of Economic Dynamics*. 41(July): pp. 225–242. https://www.sciencedirect.com/science/article/abs/pii/S1094202520301150.

Fonda, D. 2022. Solana Could Be the Visa of Crypto Networks. Not So Fast, Says Visa. *Barron's*. 13 July. https://www.barrons.com/articles/solana-could-be-the-visa-of-crypto-networks-not-so-fast-says-visa-51642091862.

Fortune Business Insights. 2022. *Market Research Report*. https://www.fortunebusinessinsights.com/industry-reports/cryptocurrency-market-100149.

Garratt, R., M. Lee, B. Malone, and A. Martin. 2020. Token- or Account-Based? A Digital Currency Can Be Both. Federal Reserve Bank of New York. *Liberty Street Economics*. 12 August. https://libertystreeteconomics.newyorkfed.org/2020/08/token-or-account-based-a-digital-currency-can-be-both/.

Hunter, S., and S. Taylor. 2020. *Enabling Shared Prosperity through Inclusive Finance: Leaving No One Behind in an Age of Disruption*. Foundation for Development Cooperation. Kenmore, Queensland. https://www2.abaconline.org/assets/2020_APFIF_FINAL_REPORT_1.pdf.

ING. 2020. *Central Bank Digital Currencies: Challenges for Commercial Banks*. 16 June. https://think.ing.com/articles/central-bank-digital-currencies-challenges-for-commercial-banks.

International Monetary Fund (IMF). 2020. *Digital Money across Borders: Macro-Financial Implications*. Washington, DC: IMF.

Jones, M. 2022. Over $315,000 in Digital Yuan Used Every Day at Olympics, PBOC Official Says. *Reuters*. 15 February. https://www.reuters.com/technology/around-300-mln-digital-yuan-used-every-day-olympics-pboc-official-says-2022-02-15/.

J.P. Morgan. 2021. *J.P. Morgan Releases Unlocking $120 billion in Cross-Border Payments Report*. 3 November. https://www.jpmorgan.com/news/jpmorgan-central-bank-digital-currency-report.

Kapronasia. 2022. Thailand Bans Crypto Payments with an Eye on a Digital Baht. 29 March. https://www.kapronasia.com/blockchain-research-menu-item/thailand-bans-crypto-payments-with-an-eye-on-a-digital-baht.html?utm_campaign=Newsletter%20Q1%202022&utm_medium=email&_hsmi=208550232&_hsenc=p2ANqtz-8eV79qEtWK2x9QmPOcKFBvKTQIDUm5ly8kLfzBlV364GVpBvdn3b58HS3lrSduYoBizVHT87qfxx1u_D3rU1omokyBVouikMHL4A0qaFO9oaMBiCg&utm_content=208550232&utm_source=hs_email.

Khiaonarong, T., and D. Humphrey. 2022. Falling Use of Cash and Demand for Retail Central. *IMF Working Papers.* No. 2022/27. Washington, DC. https://www.imf.org/-/media/Files/Publications/WP/2022/English/wpiea2022027-print-pdf.ashx.

Kiff, M.J., J. Alwazir, S. Davidovic, A. Farias, M.A. Khan, M.T. Khiaonarong, M. Malaika, H.K. Monroe, N. Sugimoto, H. Tourpe, and P. Zhou. 2020. A Survey of Research on Retail Central Bank Digital Currency. *IMF Working Papers.* No. 2020/104.

Nelms, T.C., and S.C. Rea. 2017. Mobile Money: The First Decade. *Institute for Money, Technology & Financial Inclusion Working Paper.* No. 2017-1. University of California, Irvine. https://escholarship.org/uc/item/574243f9.

Organisation for Economic Co-operation and Development (OECD). 2020. *Taxing Virtual Currencies: An Overview of Tax Treatments and Emerging Tax Policy Issues.* Paris: OECD. https://www.oecd.org/tax/tax-policy/taxing-virtual-currencies-an-overview-of-tax-treatments-and-emerging-tax-policy-issues.htm.

Pinsent Masons. 2018. *'Digital Bank Run' a Risk Should Central Banks Issue Their Own Virtual Currency, Says Weidmann.* 19 February. https://www.pinsentmasons.com/out-law/news/digital-bank-run-a-risk-should-central-banks-issue-their-own-virtual-currency-says-weidmann.

Richards, T., C. Thompson, and C. Dark. 2020. Retail Central Bank Digital Currency: Design Considerations, Rationales and Implications. *Working Paper.* Reserve Bank of Australia. Sydney. https://www.rba.gov.au/publications/bulletin/2020/sep/pdf/retail-central-bank-digital-currency-design-considerations-rationales-and-implications.pdf.

Rutkowski, M., A.G. Mora, G.L. Bull, B. Guermazi, and C. Grown. 2020. Responding to Crisis with Digital Payments for Social Protection: Short-Term Measures with Long-Term Benefits. *World Bank Blogs.* 31 March. https://blogs.worldbank.org/voices/responding-crisis-digital-payments-social-protection-short-term-measures-long-term-benefits.

Scorer, S. 2017. Beyond Blockchain: What Are the Technology Requirements for a Central Bank Digital Currency? *Bank Underground.* 13 September. https://bankunderground.co.uk/2017/09/13/beyond-blockchain-what-are-the-technology-requirements-for-a-central-bank-digital-currency/.

Sier, J. 2022. How Central Banks Are Jumping on the Crypto Bandwagon. *Financial Review.* 16 March. https://www.afr.com/technology/the-abcs-of-cbdcs-central-bank-digital-currencies-explained-20220315-p5a4sm.

Soderberg, G., M. Bechara, W. Bossu, N.X. Che, S. Davidovic, J. Kiff, I. Lukonga, T.M. Griffoli, T. Sun, and A. Yoshinaga. 2022. Behind the Scenes of Central Bank Digital Currency. *FinTech Notes.* No. 2022/004. Washington, DC: International Monetary Fund.

Soni, S. 2022. CBDCs Could Help Reduce Settlement Cycles, Enable Better Cashflow Predictions for MSMEs: Report. *Financial Express.* 9 March. https://www.financialexpress.com/industry/sme/msme-tech-cbdcs-could-help-reduce-settlement-cycles-enable-better-cashflow-predictions-for-msmes-report/2455804/.

Sridhar, N., and P. Horan. 2021. Should Central Banks Offer the Public Token-Based Digital Currencies? *Disclosure.* 8 June. Mercatus Center at George Mason University. https://www.discourse magazine.com/economics/2021/06/08/should-central-banks-offer-the-public-token-based-digital-currencies/.

United Nations Development Programme (UNDP). 2019. *Why the World Needs "Good" Digital ID.* 1 July. https://undp.medium.com/why-the-world-needs-good-digital-id-81d5688a3b68.

United Nations Social and Economic Commission for Asia and the Pacific (UNESCAP). 2022. *Policy Guidebook: Harnessing Digital Technology for Financial Inclusion in Asia and the Pacific.* Bangkok: UNESCAP. https://www.unescap.org/kp/2022/policy-guidebook-harnessing-digital-technology-financial-inclusion-asia-and-pacific-0.

Ward, O., and S. Rochemont. 2019. *Understanding Central Bank Digital Currencies (CBDC).* Institute and Faculty of Actuaries. https://www.actuaries.org.uk/system/files/field/document/Understanding%20CBDCs%20Final%20-%20disc.pdf.

World Bank. 2021. Remittances to Reach $630 billion in 2022 with Record Flows into Ukraine. News release. 11 May. https://www.worldbank.org/en/news/press-release/2022/05/11/remittances-to-reach-630-billion-in-2022-with-record-flows-into-ukraine.